Choosing Character

Choosing Character

Responsibility for Virtue and Vice

JONATHAN JACOBS

Cornell University Press

ITHACA AND LONDON

First published 2001 by Cornell University Press

Printed in the United States of America

Library of Congress Cataloging-in-Publication Data

Jacobs, Jonathan A.
　　Choosing character : responsibility for virtue and vice / Jonathan Jacobs.
　　　p. cm.
　　Includes bibliographical references and index.
　　ISBN 0-8014-3859-4　(alk. paper)
　　1. Responsibility.　2. Free will and determinism.　3. Character.
I. Title.
　　BJ1451 .J33 2001
　　170—dc21

00-012990

Cornell University Press strives to use environmentally responsible suppliers and materials to the fullest extent possible in the publishing of its books. Such materials include vegetable-based, low-VOC inks, and acid-free papers that are recycled, totally chlorine-free, or partly composed of nonwood fibers. Books that bear the logo of the FSC (Forest Stewardship Council) use paper taken from forests that have been inspected and certified as meeting the highest standards for environmental and social responsibility. For further information, visit our website at www.cornellpress.cornell.edu.

Cloth printing　　　　　　10 9 8 7 6 5 4 3 2 1

For Nancy,
Nathan and Daniel

Contents

Preface

The issue of whether vicious agents are rational and responsible is a long-standing difficulty in ethical theorizing and practice. In this book I offer a reconsideration of the extent to which agents can effectively acquire a correct grasp of ethical considerations and guide their actions by it. This involves exploring a number of topics in moral psychology and metaethics as well as the nature of voluntariness.

There appear to be strong reasons in favor of concluding that agents who lack sound understanding of ethical requirements are less than fully rational and perhaps also less than fully responsible. Nonetheless, it also seems that there are vicious agents who know what they are doing, are acting voluntarily, and who merit ascriptions of full-fledged responsibility and liability to blame. This is so even if, given their characters and circumstances, they could not have known or acted otherwise. Think of the deeply vicious agent who has an opportunity to do harm in just the way he cruelly enjoys. Not only does it not occur to him to refrain, but the reasons to refrain may not be acknowledged by him in any practically effective way. Still, he seems to be a voluntary agent enacting values he endorses.

I argue that it is not true in a completely general way that 'ought' implies 'can.' There are agents who cannot do what they ought to do, but the conditions that explain their disability do not defeat their responsibility. The account does not eliminate the perplexities we feel concerning vicious agents. It attempts to diagnose them and keep them at the center of our attention. They cannot be explained away or analytically reduced to something more amenable.

Some of the claims and arguments in the book are developments of ideas I first presented in articles. I am grateful to the editors of the journals in which those articles appear for permission to use portions of them. "Taking Ethical Disability Seriously" appeared in *Ratio*; "The

Virtues of Externalism" in the *Southern Journal of Philosophy*; "Plasticity and Perfection: Maimonides and Aristotle on Character" in *Religious Studies*; and "Luck and Retribution" in *Philosophy*. "Metaethics and Teleology" is forthcoming in the *Review of Metaphysics* at the time this book is going to press.

A large portion of the book was written during a sabbatical semester and summer spent at the University of Edinburgh and at Oxford. That sabbatical was generously supported by the Earhart Foundation, which awarded me a Fellowship Research Grant. I am very grateful to the Foundation. I also owe thanks to the Humanities Division at Colgate University for a Faculty Development Grant during that period.

While in Edinburgh I was the John MacMurray Visiting Professor of Philosophy. The department was very welcoming, and I gained a great deal by being able to spend time with its members. I offered a seminar on the metaethics of virtue, and the postgraduates and faculty who attended were generous, patient, and demanding in exemplary ways. In particular, I thank Dory Scaltsas (then Head of the Philosophy Department), David Robinson (of the Classics Faculty), and David Carr (of the Department of Educational Theory) for making the seminar a success and a pleasure. At Oxford, I was Visiting Senior Member of Linacre College, and I am very grateful to the College and especially to a very good friend there, Simon Saunders.

The book was completed while I was a Visiting Fellow at the Centre for Philosophy and Public Affairs in the Department of Moral Philosophy at the University of St. Andrews during spring 2000. For making that semester a fine experience in many ways I am especially indebted to John Haldane and David Archard. John Skorupski, Garrett Cullity, and John Broome are also owed thanks that I am very happy to extend to them.

Robert Audi of the University of Nebraska and Daniel Frank of the University of Kentucky made many helpful criticisms and suggestions in conversations and in correspondence on topics discussed in the book.

The editor at Cornell University Press, Catherine Rice, helped me in sustained, constructive, and encouraging ways. It was a pleasure to work with her. Readers for the Press did the sort of thoughtful, responsible job that made their criticism both challenging and welcome. Thanks are owed to Teresa Jesionowski, the senior manuscript editor, and Kristin Herbert, the copyeditor, for their corrections, suggestions, and indulgence. The index was prepared by Alex Jeffers, and I am indeed very grateful to him.

JONATHAN JACOBS

Hamilton, New York

Choosing Character

Introduction

The main claims of this book are that there are substantial respects in which character is voluntary, that there is an important role for character in ethical cognition, and that agents are typically responsible for their actions even when fixity of character limits what are real, practical possibilities for them. In several respects the account is a development of some Aristotelian resources, but the project is not to ascertain precisely Aristotle's own views. An important result of the account is that there are agents I shall call *ethically disabled*. Their characters are such that sound ethical considerations are inaccessible to them and they have severely limited capacity for ethical self-correction. Still, they are fully agents, and it is appropriate to attribute responsibility to them.

The phenomenon of ethical disability needs fuller treatment than it has received. Moral philosophers have not ignored vice and the ways in which we corrupt our own characters. Still, the treatment of these issues is often somewhat derivative in the sense that they are handled as departures from virtue or lapses from principles of right action. We tend to interpret what it is to be a rational agent in terms of what it is to be a well-ordered rational agent. That is fair enough; we are rational beings and rationality is indeed normative. Still, it is important to explain why and how an agent can be a responsible, rational agent and a full participant in the practical order, while being deeply alienated from what virtue requires. Such an agent does not regard himself as lapsing or violating principles of right action, and it may not be possible to change his view though he is rational. Human beings are creatures of habit, and we will see how habits for which we are responsible can be enabling in regard to virtue and how they can be disabling without creating exemption from responsibility.

1

Chapter 1 presents the view that (typically) there is a significant degree of voluntariness in the establishment of character even though everyone is subject to powerful influences of many kinds. I do not mean that agents choose their characteristics, but that the way in which the exercise of voluntariness is involved in the formation of character supplies grounds for regarding agents as responsible for many of their ethically relevant characteristics. Even the very young, who do not yet act on the basis of practical reasoning, move about voluntarily and there is not some particular point or stage of life at which one *becomes* a voluntary agent. There is voluntariness all along, but the texture of it changes. There is voluntary motion that developmentally precedes rational, deliberate motion, and the character of one's voluntariness changes with maturity. The agent becomes more capable of rational judgment and is more in control of what appears good. Responsibility increases accordingly.

Habituation has a powerful formative influence on character. There are, though, ways in which being habituated involves the agent's own voluntariness. It certainly does in so far as compliance and willingness are involved. Even though a good deal of habituation occurs prior to the time the agent is rationally mature, it is still not a process that simply imposes characteristics. Moreover, as one matures, habituation is more and more a process of habituating *oneself* as there is a greater role for one's own reasons, judgment, and perspective in motivating actions and shaping dispositions. The establishment of a characteristic is rarely if ever the effect of any single action or decision, though voluntary acts have the cumulative effect of shaping character. Thus, in addition to pre-rational habituation there are also the habits that mature agents establish in themselves, and the latter are of particular importance in this account. Habituation is not exclusively something that only goes on (or that 'happens to' a person) during a stage of life prior to when he or she is capable of practical reasoning. It is also a process we engage in by acting on the basis of what we take to be good reasons for action and what we judge to be worthwhile and desirable.

While the interpretation of voluntariness is important to the overall account, the free will debate is not the central concern here. Rather than attempting to resolve the metaphysical issue of free will and determinism, I pursue some avenues that explanatorily relate important issues of moral psychology and moral cognition. I am more concerned with various issues connected with what agents 'have to' (or cannot) do on account of character as a matter of moral psychology than with determinism as a metaphysical issue. The views defended are at odds with hard determinism but do not require that determinism is false, only that determinist incompatibilism is false.

The discussion of responsibility for character shows that agents can voluntarily come to be ethically disabled. This is the main topic of chapter 2. A rationally competent agent may voluntarily come to have a character such that it is not practically possible for that person to recognize ethical considerations in the right sort of way and to be motivated by them. These agents are still responsible for their actions despite the fact that their conceptions of value may be so disordered that well-ordered practical comprehension and reasoning are no longer realistic possibilities for them.[1] At least these are not things that it would be reasonable to expect of these agents.

An agent can come to be ethically disabled voluntarily without having set out to become so just as one can voluntarily come to lead an unhappy life without having unhappiness as an aim. The agent does not engage in actions under the description 'doing this, or doing this regularly, is likely to cause a undesirable limitation of my judgmental or motivational capacities.' Still, the agent's voluntary actions have that effect, and the agent may even have some awareness of it. So the agent acts voluntarily and knowingly in ways that degrade his ethical personality, though he is not aiming to do so. (Or, he may have been warned but does not believe or heed the warning.) I argue that even the influence of ethically disordered prevailing norms and perspectives generally does not excuse the agent's responsibility or lessen the voluntariness of his character. That claim is central to this book and thematically unifies the overall discussion.

The issue of whether there is such a state as ethical disability *matters* for a number of reasons. It bears on questions about what can be reasonably expected of people with respect to sound moral understanding and the capacity to reform unsound understanding and dispositions. Is a developed, effective ability to understand ethical matters in a sound manner a necessary condition for attributing moral responsibility? (I will answer in the negative.) Can mature, rational agents be morally incorrigible? (I will answer in the affirmative.) Ethical disability also bears on the extent to which moral disagreements can be resolved by reflection and reasoning. There may well be agents who are rational and responsible but who are impervious to right reason with respect to various ethical matters. They are not incompetent as rational agents but they are in certain important respects, unreachable. I think that there are such agents and that their actions and characters make for a kind of unclarity on the ethical landscape. We are often perplexed about how to address these agents and what attitudes and actions are appropriate with regard to them. To resolve the unclarity by diminishing their responsibility might make our ethics more tidy, but it would be a kind of denial, a denial of the fullness of their voluntary agency and participation with us in a common ethical world.

The notion of ethical disability is also relevant to the debate about the appropriate weights of retributive, deterrent, expressive, rehabilitative, and denunciatory considerations in conceptions of the justification and aims of punishment. (I am beginning to explore these issues in a fuller way in other work).[2] I will not explore the issue of punishment here on a large scale, though I will make some remarks about the ethical aptness of retributivist considerations in general and suggest how the issue of ethical disability might bear on retributivist considerations in the justification of punishment.

There surely are agents who generally act in conformity with what morality and the law require while not having ethical integrity or admirable character. Perhaps they are just being prudent or perhaps they have had the experience of blame and punishment and want no more of it. They may also just be reliable moral conformists, as it were. My main concern though, is to show that even agents who endorse wrong or perverse values and who cannot see the wrongness or perversity of them may well be responsible agents, and I am not exclusively concerned with the issue of moral responsibility in a narrow sense. I think that there is a point in noting a distinction between moral requirements and a broader notion of ethics, though it is exceedingly difficult to make the distinction in a hard and fast way. The latter concerns agents' valuative attachments and perspectives and conduct of life generally, whereas the former more narrowly concerns how one acts with regard to others, and is a less broad matter of evaluating agents with respect to their excellences and defects. The issues of moral psychology taken up here mainly concern what I just identified as ethics rather than the more verdictive and (at least in form) legalistic issues of morality. The question "What does a theory of morally right behavior require?" is a quite different question from "To what extent are agents properly responsible for the valuative attachments and motivational policies that shape their characters and actions?" The relation between this kind of responsibility and more narrowly defined moral responsibility is a complex and important one. However, to get a purchase on it, we need first to give a general account of the responsibility of agents in the broader ethical sense.[3]

In chapter 3 I try to show more fully why the role of character in ethical cognition has the result that we should be modest in our expectations that certain sorts of agents are capable of ethical reform. This chapter addresses the issue of the extent to which mature agents can revise their characters in ethically significant ways. The focus is sharpened by examining some of the views of Maimonides and contrasting them with the account so far.

Maimonides is a profound but neglected thinker whose moral psychology is in many ways much like Aristotle's, but he allows for the possibility of reform of character to an extent that Aristotle does not. His views can be used to delineate some helpful contrasts *within* a broadly Aristotelian framework. That is the main reason they are discussed. Unlike Kant, he does not hold that there is one fundamental principle of right action constructed by practical reason. (He is like Aristotle on that score.) Unlike Mill, he does not hold that there is one fundamental criterion of right action ascertainable by consideration of some general facts about human nature. (He is like Aristotle on that score.) Unlike Aquinas, he does not hold that there is an innate disposition to grasp first principles of practical reason. But Maimonides does maintain that what is ethically required is not inaccessible, even to the bad man, and that someone long-established in vice can effectively ethically self-correct. This is where he and Aristotle differ. They agree on a great deal concerning habituation, the acquisition of the virtues and vices, and the voluntariness of states of character. The discussion will reveal how different interpretations of the objectivity of ethical considerations are related to different interpretations of moral psychology and the capacity for changing one's ethically significant dispositions.

Even though Maimonides is a religious thinker, his account of repentance and reform of character does not involve supernatural grace or any intervening agency or power other than one's own will.[4] He has a theistic view of ethical objectivity but a naturalistic view of the possibility of altering character. His works show us what a basically Aristotelian moral psychology looks like when the power of will is enlarged so that it can revise mature character. So, even though Maimonides is not widely known, he supplies us with an outstandingly clear example of the relation between the accessibility of ethical considerations and the plasticity of character that I wish to explore. The examination of his view will help articulate ethical disability. If the arguments of chapters 1 and 2 succeed, then we will have support to claim that it is not the case that "ought implies can" for all rational agents, and that it is not always true that "the agent could have known better" is a condition of responsibility. These are among the most important results of the account.

Chapter 4 is a discussion of conscience. Perhaps if each agent has a conscience in the way it is understood in some traditional theories, that would be a reason to think that agents do not really become ethically disabled or at least that they are capable of ethical self-correction. They would have a capacity or a faculty that enables them to grasp fundamental practical principles or correct values and that also has a special kind of action-guiding authority. Certainly if conscience is innate or essentially connected with rationality there might be the resources in every agent to judge rightly and perhaps even to reform character in the direction of virtue. I shall argue that while the main traditional conceptions of conscience express important features of ethical life and phenomenology, conscience is not a faculty or power in the ways that it is often taken to be. In explicating this claim, the views of Butler, Kant, and Aquinas (and some others) will be discussed. There will be no suggestion that we should abandon the idiom of conscience. However, the wide range of phenomena referred to by it can be explained and understood in terms of features of the acquired second natures of agents.

The defense of ethical realism in chapter 5 completes the presentation of the main elements of the account. It is not a full-scale presentation of metaethical theory. Rather, it is there to help explicate the moral psychology that is the central concern of the book. We will see again that the interpretation of habits is important. Among the most important positions in contemporary metaethics are a basically Humean position and a basically Aristotelian position, and one of the key differences between them is how they interpret habits of ethical thought and the extent to which they are habits of *cognition*. I defend a basically Aristotelian interpretation of habits of ethical cognition, and try to show why it should be regarded as a realist interpretation. The moral psychological claims do not require a realist metaethic but the moral psychology and the metaethic are mutually reinforcing in ways I shall indicate.

In the conclusion the main claims of the book are recapitulated, and the most important connections between them are restated and reinforced. In particular, I discuss the respect in which the claims about virtue and the way in which virtue is naturally pleasing do not require that there should be an innate disposition to pursue what is good or an innate capacity for vicious agents to reconnect with the good. Agents find habits pleasing, and this is true of both virtuous and vicious agents. The pleasure that accompanies acting in ways that are second nature has a central role in moral psychology. Reflection on the phenomenology of habit and on the relation between pleasure and an agent's conception of what is good reveal limitations on the accessibility of ethical considerations to an established second nature. These limitations suggest ways in which many approaches to moral theory are implausibly optimistic if a broadly Aristotelian naturalism is true.

I conclude here with a remark about method. There are different ways of philosophically showing something. One method is to formulate truth-conditions. Another is to examine concepts and issues in a detailed manner with the aim of clarifying them and their relations, which is the method I've employed. By bringing into view an overall conception of responsibility for character, ethical cognition, and ethical objectivity, I hope to illuminate explanatory relations between them, and, in particular, identify and explicate ethical disability. I have not attempted to formulate necessary and sufficient conditions, for "act A, performed by agent X at t, in circumstances C, is voluntary" or "X's character at t_1 is different from X's character at t'." Rather than separating out one or another thread for complete analysis, I have tried to bring into view the pattern in a large fabric of conceptions about human action, responsibility, and ethical value.

CHAPTER 1

Voluntariness and Habits

Everybody has a story, and one's background and circumstances are key components of it. Although we might expect the complete account, the 'whole story,' to be very complex, sometimes a particular element is identified as a key to it. Perhaps it is the socioeconomic context of upbringing. It might be the fact that a parent was a depressed alcoholic with a volatile temper. Maybe it is the fact the individual is a member of a group that has suffered exclusion and persecution, or has undergone considerable emotional suffering, and so forth. Perhaps it is the fact that the person never had to work and look after his own affairs in a responsible manner. Temperament too, is a crucial element. Qualities such as timidity and aggressiveness, or patience and anxiousness, and so forth are natural features that give contour to one's character and agency. An individual's story is shot through with luck of various kinds, internal and external, and coming from all directions. This is not luck in the sense of randomness, but in the sense that there is so much about each of us and about our situations that is not directly or fully under our control. This includes our physiology, natural propensities and abilities, the situations and challenges we face, and the people who affect our lives. There is little question that the more knowledge we have of such matters, the better able we are to make sense of someone's character and actions. Still, there remain reasons to reserve a centrally important role for voluntariness in action and in the leading of a life, and a correspondingly substantial role for responsibility with respect to character.

THE BREADTH OF VOLUNTARINESS

When a child chases after a balloon she has let go of she is acting voluntarily. So are her parents when, after careful deliberation, they decide to send her to one pre-school rather than another. A great deal of human activity is voluntary in the sense that it is uncompelled, the agent is doing what she wants to do, and the agent is aware of, and has some measure of control over what she is doing. This, I believe, expresses a plausible core conception of voluntariness, and it applies to a broad range of human action, from early ages up through adult action guided by deliberative exercises of practical reason. Of course, it is not simply obvious that if there are voluntary actions, then character too is voluntary. There are, though, reasons based upon the voluntariness of human action that do support the view that there are substantial respects in which character is voluntary and that agents are responsible for their characters.[1] The discussion of those reasons, especially with respect to habituation, will be the basis for the subsequent discussions of ethical disability, the possibility of character change, and conscience.

We typically think of ourselves and of others as voluntary, responsible agents. This is not in itself evidence for the truth of a thesis about freedom of the will, but neither is it something that can be ignored or dismissed because it is, say, unscientific.[2] When we ask "What is she up to these days?" or "Why did he leave that job?" or "How is he handling things since the accident?" and the like, there is a presumption that those being asked about are responsible as agents of their acts, even as we recognize the significance of circumstances and other influencing factors. Our interest in those individuals may be motivated by knowledge that something has happened to them or for them, but what we want to know is what they are making of their situations and what they are doing about them. That concern reflects the way in which we (correctly) regard older children, adolescents, and adults as participants in a practical order, a world of agents who have conceptions of what they are doing, who are generally not compelled, and who are thought of as responsible unless there are special reasons not to think so.

I will argue that this presumption is true with respect to responsibility for both character and actions. Gregory Trianosky writes of ascriptions of responsibility for character that their point is "not to establish that one formed one's character freely, or even that one could have 'done otherwise,' developed some other character instead. The point is to establish that of the various persons who might have authored your character, you were the one who did and not someone else. The content of your character is to be explained by the activity of your agency, and not by the activity of some other agent. It is for this reason too that faced with the inelim-inable influence of constitutive luck on character, we find the option of abandoning ascriptions of responsibility for character altogether unat-tractive. To do so is to abandon a significant portion of the attempt to understand one's life as one's own."[3] We can acknowledge the role of influences, background, circumstances, and the like without abandoning the conception of people as voluntary agents. Although more and more is being discovered about the various causal influences on action and char-acter, this does not provide adequate grounds to nullify significant ascrip-tions of voluntariness and responsibility.

These discoveries may motivate important revisions in how we under-stand some behaviors. For example, if it is found that there is a significant genetic factor in obesity or alcoholism or other conditions and disposi-tions, we should adjust the way we regard those who have them (with respect to blame, patience, sympathy, vigilance, therapeutic strategies, etc.). The ever more numerous discoveries of nonvoluntary and congeni-tal factors across a vast range of human propensities and dispositions should inform and guide attributions of responsibility rather than elimi-nate them. For example, we should distinguish between those who are alcoholic or obese in large part *because of* the predisposition and those who are alcoholic or obese but lack the predisposition. Moreover, a pre-disposition on its own is not a compelling cause, and there is a good deal of variability that needs to be acknowledged with respect to attributions of responsibility even where there are underlying propensities the agent has not had a role in shaping. We need clarity about the roles and relations of temperament, practical reason, and valuative commitments as much as we need more accurate causal knowledge.

I remarked above that 'the voluntary' is a notion with quite wide appli-cability. One merit of a broadly Aristotelian interpretation of voluntari-ness is that it is not confined to acts flowing from deliberation or decision. (See, for example, *NE* 1111a 26 and 1112a15.) Aristotle's discussion of vol-untariness recognizes developmental changes in the character of it with the increasing involvement of the agent's reasoning abilities and recog-nizes the overall continuity of juvenile voluntariness with adult voluntari-ness.[4] Along with the enlargement of the range of voluntary activities in which the maturing agent can engage, come appropriately enlarged attri-butions of responsibility.

We are accustomed to calibrating attributions of responsibility on the basis of the extent to which it is appropriate to expect agents to be aware of what they are doing and the extent to which reason, decision, and understanding can be expected to inform their actions.[5] Thus, with respect to an adolescent or a grown-up, but not with respect to a very young child, it makes sense to investigate whether negligence, mitigating, or aggravating conditions were involved. With maturation we expect an increasing knowledge of particulars and an enlarged general awareness of what is acceptable, what invites recrimination, anger, gratitude, or admiration, and so forth. The notion of 'the voluntary' is thereby applicable to all of the following. (1) A four-year-old dropping his jacket (again) on the floor upon coming into the house. (2) A twelve-year-old smoking a cigarette in response to a dare. (3) A twenty-year-old cursing at another driver. (4) A fifty-five year-old offering her son-in-law money to help keep his business solvent.

We can illustrate some of the relations between responsibility and knowledge of what one is doing with the following example. Suppose you set about throwing out old receipts, paid bills, catalogues, and the like. As you go through the envelopes in the desk drawer, you see that there are two dozen old telephone bills that have surely been paid. You check the five most recent and find that indeed they have been paid, and proceed to discard them and all of the older ones (without looking in the rest of the envelopes). You do not know that in one of the envelopes there are some love letters that a member of the household has hidden there because, of course, no one is expected to look through all those old envelopes. You throw out the envelope with the letters (without having looked in it). When it is discovered that the letters are missing, you are accused of throwing them away. You explain that you did not know of their existence, never laid eyes or hands on them, and of course would not have discarded them, or even have read them, if you had discovered them. Your act is the cause of the loss of the letters, but responsibility (in the sense of blameworthiness) is defeated by your excusable ignorance. You did not throw them out voluntarily, though you were cleaning out the desk voluntarily.

There are aspects of agency in this case that are absent in the example of, say, a baby trying to walk and knocking over a standing lamp in the attempt. Those different aspects have to do with the capacity for deliberate action, foresight, self-awareness, and evaluation of the ends and means of action. The baby's walking and your tidying-up are both voluntary. Neither the breaking of the lamp nor the destruction of the letters is voluntary, though the explanation of why in the case concerning the letters points to factors not present in the other case. The character of voluntariness needs to be more and more carefully specified as the agent is a more rationally capable agent with different types of awareness and knowledge expected at different levels of maturity.

Even very young children are capable of voluntary motion, and this is not on account of having deliberated about what to do or on account of any distinctive interior act of will. The baby who learns to roll over can then do so because it wants to, but it is not always an explicit intention that makes an act voluntary. It is doubtful that a six-month-old, for example, has the artic-ulate, self-conscious thought "Rolling over seems to be the thing to do right now." Still less likely does the baby think that it is the thing to do because "they'll love it." Yet, the rolling over is not just like laughing when being tickled. The baby moves voluntarily though it is not action for which the baby is responsible in any morally interesting sense. We might however, encourage the behavior as a way of helping the baby develop and as a mode of playful interaction. (It can be *practically* interesting behavior even if not *morally* interesting.) In fact, even for adults there is a great deal of voluntary motion that does not involve much in the way of explicit judgment or delib-eration. Turning over on the sofa to get more comfortable is voluntary and so is rubbing one's eyes after taking off glasses.

The young child does not, at some specific point in development, *become* capable of voluntary motion. Rather, the child becomes capable of different kinds of voluntary motion at different points. The baby who rolls over to get closer to a toy is moving voluntarily. So is the four-year-old who dropped his jacket on the floor upon coming into the house. In the latter case there is a place for considerations about responsibility, supposing he has been told not to just drop his jacket; he can be expected to acquire the habit of putting it away. In that instance, there are some of the ele-ments of practical comprehension, and the child has some grasp of reward and punishment and the reality and significance of the approval and displeasure of others. They are not just forces in the environment in the way that they might be to an infant. They are part of a social world that he has begun to understand himself to be living in. With respect to the activity of mature, rational agents, their manner of engaging with the world, their conceptions of what to aim at and why are crucial to the explanation of their actions.

HABITUATION

By the time we become mature, self-conscious practical reason-ers, we have already acquired some quite firm dispositions concerning what sorts of considerations count with respect to choosing, acting, and reacting. We have some settled ends and some settled patterns of motiva-tion. If there were not a substantial role for voluntariness in the formation of those dispositions, it would be very unclear indeed how one could be responsible for character and for what appears good.

Given the emphasis that Aristotle puts on habituation (see, e.g., *NE* 1095b5–10, 1103a16, 1103b24–25) it might seem that the claim that char-acter is substantially voluntary has already been undermined. Bernard

Williams, for example, argues that "Aristotle should not have believed that in the most basic respects, at least, people were responsible for their characters. He gives an account of moral development in terms of habituation and internalization that leaves little room for practical reason to alter radically the objectives that a grown-up person has acquired."[6]

It may be true that once one's character is quite firmly established there is not much prospect of it being radically changed or even much prospect of the agent being motivated to try to significantly alter his character. After all, given one's established states of character, there are significant limitations on how one is likely to see things and be motivated. (Much of Williams's own work has explored the centrality of character in practical reasoning and the ways in which the boundaries of what one can do are shaped by character.)[7] Bad luck with respect to the development of one's practical vision and motivational dispositions is not easily overcome, and good luck is a significant advantage. However, there is a substantial role for voluntariness in being habituated and in explaining why habituation and luck (for better or worse) do not diminish responsibility for character. In fact, I believe the claim that in substantial respects character is voluntary is not only true, but is *supported* by what Aristotle says about habit. The main concern here is not interpreting Aristotle, but we can see where the support is if we have a notion of habit adequate to the breadth of voluntariness in the way Aristotle does. We will follow this up in a moment.

Still, it is not hard to see why Williams arrived at the conclusion indicated above. In the *Nicomachean Ethics* the focus is on habituation by encouragement and discouragement, and the shaping of dispositions to find activities pleasing or painful. The virtues, Aristotle says, are not present in us by nature; "but we are by nature able to acquire them, and reach our complete perfection through habit" (*NE* 1103a25). And, "it is not unimportant, then, to acquire one sort of habit or another, right from our youth; rather, it is very important, indeed all-important" (*NE* 1103b24-25). And "good or bad enjoyment or pain is very important for our actions" (*NE* 1105a7). These passages are indicative of the significance Aristotle assigns to habituation with respect to formation of character, and they can give the impression that habituation largely fixes character. They also make it sound as though there is little role for the agent's own deliberation in how he is habituated. This could lead us to conclude that a mature individual's practical reasoning is shaped by valuative notions and dispositions that in turn were formed by something other than that individual's voluntariness. What considerations are there in the way of this conclusion?

On the present interpretation of voluntariness, and, I believe, on Aristotle's, acquiring habits is (or at least, often is) voluntary. As Richard

Sorabji observes, "in childhood, when habits are being formed, the intellect is still immature, and children are naturally obedient."[8] Nevertheless, "Aristotle is not obliged to treat the discipline of parents as an external origin in the sense which he had in mind in *NE* III 1. For one thing, as we saw, that was three times described as an external origin which operates *without the agent contributing anything*. In the present case, the child must contribute something. At a minimum, he contributes the will to comply or the refusal. This can be important; if we recall the case of the child attracted by a toy which he knows he is forbidden to take, it may be up to him which course he follows."[9]

In large part, the voluntariness of one's characteristics can be explained in terms of the fact that the actions that caused one's dispositions had their origin in the agent's voluntary (even if strongly encouraged or guided) activity. Granted, with a child or even an adolescent this voluntary behavior often involves action directed by another without the young person having initiated the act in the sense of having originated the thought on one's own to do it. Juvenile actions take place in a context of norms, reprimands, expectations, and inducements almost wholly shaped by others. In addition, the young person may not yet be able or inclined to imagine different ways of acting. Yet, even these constraints do not close off all space for voluntariness. Indeed, one reason that habituation is so important is that it is a *training of voluntariness*. Even when there is minimal deliberation and not much opportunity to act otherwise, the transmission of values occurring through habituation is occurring in an individual whose choices and acts make a difference to the extent to which the values are transmitted. The agent being habituated typically acts on his or her own desires and responses to the prompting, warnings, or suggestions of others. The most immediate objection is that the agent has so little voluntary control over his desires and responses that it can seem almost precious to assign him a role as an agent in acting on them, except by virtue of the fact that they are *his*. The objection misrepresents the situation. Even a child often has some awareness of choices and opportunities of action and reaction and exercises voluntariness in proceeding. Moreover, while the process of habituation plainly does reinforce tendencies, encourage certain attitudes, establish patterns of motivation, and in those senses it shapes characteristics, it does not supply a character to the agent. The establishment of stable, mature character involves the voluntariness and the practical reasoning of the agent, even though the 'materials' one works with are largely shaped by factors not in one's direct control. Even directed, guided activity typically involves voluntariness, and while the child is not making deliberative decisions about how to behave, neither is its behavior a mechanical result of habituation.

In the process of habituation, the individual develops rational capacities for recognition and judgment. Habituation need not fix limits on how the agent will see things and reason about them. It may educate the agent to have a subtle, discriminating, careful way of looking and thinking. Habituation can be a process that develops capacities for valuative perception and discrimination rather than narrowing them. Even at quite early stages there can be a cognitive dimension to habituation that will later be crucial to responsible, mature action. As Nancy Sherman notes: "What is required [in the process of habituation which trains the young person's reason] is a shifting of beliefs and perspectives through the guidance of an outside instructor. Such guidance cannot merely be a matter of bringing the child to see this way now but of providing some sort of continuous and consistent instruction which will allow for the formation of patterns and trends in what the child notices and sees."[10] Habit need not be an action-guiding tendency that shrinks the scope for the exercise of perception and reason. And Sorabji observes of the process of habituation: "The first thing to notice is that it is not a mindless process. If someone is to be good-tempered, he must not be habituated to avoid anger come what may. The habit he must acquire is that of avoiding anger on the right occasions and of feeling it on the right occasions. As a result, habituation involves assessing the situation and seeing what is called for."[11]

The process of habituation can appeal to the individual's rationality in certain ways except at the earliest ages (where it is still laying the groundwork for certain kinds of appeals to reason later on). An eight-year-old can acquire a more meaning-laden appreciation of the importance of controlling his temper, or waiting his turn, or being grateful than just by being muscled into following rules or being threatened with punishment. There is a role for awakening understanding and the consideration of one's own motives. These are, of course, in very preliminary and undeveloped form. Nonetheless, even early habituation can begin the process of integrating beliefs, desires, and passions in ways that can then be more fully elaborated by the individual who is being habituated as his rational capacities are more fully and widely exercised.

Habit is a notion of much more than action directed by another before one is capable of mature practical reasoning. Habit, like voluntariness, extends across the full range of action from the pre-rational to the fully deliberative. The emphasis on habit in Book II of *Nicomachean Ethics* stresses the early, predeliberative ordering of desire. That emphasis is wholly appropriate. With maturity, though, capabilities for more critical and self-critical directing of action are enlarged. One never has a will unconditioned by one's own past history of action, choice, and response, but the character of one's activity changes with increased experience, more developed rationality, and awareness of the difference made by one's actions to oneself and others. There is no intrinsic opposition between having been habituated and being a fully voluntary, deliberating agent.

We noted that much of the learning that shapes deliberative capacities comes through being habituated, and our actions, though expressive of habits, increasingly involve deliberation. It is certainly true that there is a contrast between doing something 'merely' or 'purely' out of habit and doing something deliberately where this involves a self-conscious process of reasoning. But the two ways of acting do not always or necessarily exclude each other. Many of the things we do habitually we do deliberately because we have come to have those habits on account of thinking that there are good reasons to act in those ways. Many of our habits (even if they are bad habits) are formed as a result of our own practical reasoning. For example, one might have a habit of regular exercise or healthy diet as a strongly established disposition of second nature and have formed it and sustained it on the basis of one's own reasoning that it is a good thing. Or, one might have a habit of checking to make sure that the neighbor's child is able to get into her house when returning from school (because her parents are at work). This person might ('from habit') find himself checking even when the neighbors are off from work, or when school is closed. This is a habit shaped by reason and not just by patterns of external inducement. A habit is something done regularly, but not everything habitual is done without thought or done as a result of conditioning that defeats voluntariness. It may be that the habits of exercise or checking on the safety of the neighbor's child are partly explained by values transmitted by others; perhaps being raised a certain way encouraged this person's concern to have a habit of responsibility. Nonetheless, it is up to the mature agent to sustain or abandon the habit and to develop a general tendency into this or that specific habit. That is a result of exercises of practical reason for which the agent is responsible. There are features of the habit of checking on the neighbor's child that plainly make it a quite different sort of habit from keeping each food item on one's plate from touching any of the others.

To illustrate some of these claims about voluntariness and responsibility consider an untypical situation. (The example is loosely based on a news report of a situation of this kind.) Imagine a young child confined (alone) to a room for three years, fed on a diet minimally adequate for subsistence, and kept from all but minimal social interaction. That does not count as a process of habituation in which there is voluntary activity and responsibility that increases with the passage of time. This may seem to differ only in degree from being raised in a household in which the prevailing influences are people who are, for instance, hot-tempered, selfish, and mean. In what respect is there voluntariness involved in the development of *either* child's character? What chance does either child have of developing in ways that escape or defy the prevailing influences on them?

The first setting is crucially different from the second due to the destruction of capacities for character caused by coercion and deprivation. In the first case, there is deprivation of experience and social interaction on a catastrophic scale. The confined child is not being habituated badly, she is being incapacitated for learning from experience, developing anything like normal emotionality, and developing the rational abilities the exercise of which merits attributions of responsibility. In the second case there are obstacles, handicaps, and unhealthy influences, but not the destruction of capacities that occurs in the first case. In the second case, the child is up against serious obstacles but does not develop as a lesser agent on account of them. Without doubt, the early influences set up patterns of motivation, evaluation, and action, but the second child will be a more fully voluntary agent as he or she matures, in spite of the unhelpful and even harmful early influences.

Consider another example, this time concerning an adult. Imagine someone with a habit of retailing gossip. This person is always keen to hear gossip and to transmit it, perhaps with embellishment or distortion. For one or another reason (perhaps finding himself on the other side of this sort of thing) he begins to feel that this is a bad practice and begins to doubt whether he should enjoy it quite as much as he does. This initiates a process of trying to break the habit, and the course this takes might be as follows. First, through an effort of self-control, he undertakes not to seek out gossip and pass on the sorts of things that before, he would have eagerly conveyed. Also, he makes an effort not to embellish as well as an effort to withdraw from this sort of conversation. It can be important not only to do less of this but also to be *recognized* as doing less of it. This person wishes to be counted on less for this sort of thing and wants not to be seen as a reliable source of gossip. If the effort at self-control succeeds he may find that with the passage of time the appetite for this activity and its pleasures diminishes and it is no longer so much a matter of restraining himself. Instead, the taste for it is gone. Maybe a strong (and even somewhat exaggerated) distaste for it has taken its place. He now regards it as a bit dangerous, something that must be avoided altogether. The desire is gone, and the pleasure is no longer missed. In fact, the agent may begin to wonder how it could *ever* have been so much enjoyed by him.

Again, we must grant that whether or not one is the sort of person who is motivated to pay this sort of attention to one's own character may have something to do with early habituation. However, whether or not the agent was habituated to have this sort of concern for his character, it would be a mistake to interpret adult practical reasoning as being fully constrained by pre-rational habituation. That would implausibly restrict the scope there is for agents to habituate themselves and to try to change their habits as they mature.

There are of course characteristics that have a grounding in temperament in such a way that it is very difficult to altogether overcome the underlying propensities. Someone may be an agitated, impatient person, or may be particularly inclined to anxiety, but not because of any pattern of habituation. We are, however, more or less able to discipline ourselves with respect to these propensities, at least with respect to how they are reflected in reasoning and judgment. The gossip may really become a 'former' gossip and lose the taste altogether, but the agitated person may have to maintain a kind of self-aware self-control without overcoming the propensity. That responsibility for character is to be ascribed to agents is not to say that they can be fully or equally responsible for all of their characteristics. The efforts one makes to be more honest, for example, are different from the efforts one makes to be less prone to fear or pessimism. It is a different sort of undertaking. The reasons for this have to do with the different 'materials' that are being worked with and on. Still, across that range and the various degrees of plasticity there is a significant role for the agent's own voluntariness and responsibility.

The upshot is that habituation is not per se a process that restricts or constrains voluntariness or that diminishes the individual's responsibility. If we think of it as a process by which dispositions are imposed upon someone, or as a process by which one's capacities for self-determination are limited, then obviously habituation will be in considerable tension with adult responsibility for character. Those readings of habituation are too narrow. We should not regard habituation as *limiting* voluntariness but as a process crucial to the development of it. Again, even if we are skeptical of there being a uniquely best actualization of human potentiality, and even if we are more pluralistic or more inclined to domesticate various kinds of value and human good to subjective projects than Aristotle was, the significance of both prerational habituation *and* rational agents' voluntarily habituating themselves is undiminished.

As we have noted, children move about voluntarily, but plainly we attribute responsibility to adults in different ways than to children, and we praise and blame them differently. It can make good sense to say to a young person "You don't want to make a habit of that," meaning something like, "There are good reasons you can and should acknowledge concerning why it is not good to become the sort of person who thinks that doing that is all right or desirable." The implied warning is that if you do that sort of thing often enough you risk becoming that sort of person, and it will be your own fault. So, for this young person there is not yet an articulate action-guiding conception of what sort of life to lead, though there is enough reason at work or available to make a rational appeal to him and for him to recognize the role of his own voluntariness.

It would, of course, be wrong to attribute to a young child a conception of his life as a whole or any sort of articulate self-conscious strategy of decision making. Obviously, these things are developed later on. But there is not some specific point at which an individual becomes a fully responsible agent. Instead, the capacities for this sort of decision and planning are developed along with and through the development of one's capacities for voluntary activity.

HABITS, AWARENESS, AND RESPONSIBILITY

In his emphasis on the role of voluntariness with respect to character, Aristotle insists that "[Only] a totally insensible person would not know that each type of activity is the source of the corresponding state" (*NE* 1114a9–11). We might question both how plausible and how fair this is. It is the sort of knowledge we might reasonably expect of an adult but not of a child. Aristotle's view (and the present view) does *not* commit the error that is found in the following conjunction of claims: (1) Early on, character becomes fixed through habituation. (2) Subsequently we are practical reasoners deliberating from premises and tendencies grounded in habits, the acquisition of which we had little or no control over. (3) We are responsible for our adult characters anyway. It should be recalled that Aristotle's conditions for the full-fledged possession of a virtue are first, that the agent "must know [that he is doing virtuous actions]; second, he must decide on them, and decide on them for themselves; and, third, *he must also do them from a firm and unchanging state*" (*NE* 1105a31–35, emphasis added). Vices too can become fixed, full-fledged features of an agent's character. The importance of this is that it is *before* one's character is fixed and unchangeable that capacities for knowing, deliberate action are developed. There is a difference between having characteristics and having a settled character. The young person has characteristics that *may* become fixed, but there is still plasticity of character that can be shaped by voluntary activity. Awareness of one's own motives and actions and the ways in which one is regarded by others is material to which an agent can respond critically in the attempt to dispose oneself in certain ways rather than others. An individual has characteristics (perhaps strongly influenced by the habituating practices of others) before settling into a more firmly fixed, mature character.

This also helps explain how there is scope for responsibility for character even though prevailing social norms and conventions play a significant role in habituation. "Prior social forms enter into our formation as persons through the activity of previously socialized caretakers, and we are sustained and tained [*sic*] as persons with certain kinds of structured identities in social relations that we help change and modify but do not in the first instance create. We are neither creators nor sole guardians of our identities. The intersubjective conception of the self is something every moral or political conception should accept."[12] The present case for voluntariness and responsibility has not tried to find a way around this. The intersubjective context is the context of human voluntariness and responsibility for character, and its influences are diverse in kind and are powerful. It is not only the context in which much of one's aspirations, attitudes, and horizons are shaped, it is also context in which one develops the rational capacities for consideration of them, elaboration and adjustment or endorsement of them, and so forth. There is shaping without this inevitably crowding out the role for the agent's practical reasoning and self-reflections with respect to settling into a mature character. Even if what the agent settles into is a kind of complacency or uncritical, unquestioning mode of life, it is what the agent, as a voluntary agent settles into. The voluntary, even in so far as it involves practical reasoning, need not be ambitious, exploratory, or reflective.

In many cases it might seem that nature and habit have conspired to write a story that ends badly, with the person having bad character. Could this person have made other kinds of judgments and come to weigh and regard matters differently? To do so might have taken courage and imagination, and it is a process that surely would have been aided by guidance and having examples to emulate. Still, we should hesitate to conclude that there is a rule of proportionality between being badly habituated and having diminished responsibility. Even the badly habituated agent is a practical reasoner, acting in accord with her own conception of good, in accord with her sense of what is desirable and her appreciation of what value things have. The agent can be a full-fledged agent, having responsibility for states of character, even if other ways of seeing things were not presented to her as equally accessible alternatives. The adult is responsible for her conception of good and for enacting it not because she authors it out of wholly self-created materials but because there is the capacity for control over what one does and what one aims to do. With the passage of time one's own attention to things and one's own consideration of wants, aims, and concerns figure more centrally in action. The transformation of habituated tendencies into firm characteristics that motivate specific actions through practical reasoning is a process in which progressively more self-controlled voluntariness is engaged.

Here an objection might be made that in order for an agent to be responsible for a characteristic, the agent must *know* that her actions will lead to the establishment of that characteristic. Otherwise, the agent did not see the characteristic 'coming.' It was not intended and not foreseen. How then, can we hold the agent responsible for it? After all, if the ignorance of the agent defeats responsibility in the throwing-out-letters case, why doesn't ignorance defeat responsibility here? To some extent this objection can be deflected by noting that the sort of knowledge in question *is* often available if the agent pays attention in certain ways. It is not specialized or technical knowledge. We do not know which drink will make us into alcoholics, and we do not know which lie will make us into liars. (There almost certainly is not *one* that does.) Still, as an agent matures, it is reasonable to enlarge the expectation that she is aware, or able to be aware, of how her acts can make a difference to her character. Aristotle remarks that "it is unreasonable [to suppose] that someone who does unjust or intemperate actions does not wish to be unjust or intemperate" (*NE* 1114a11–13). The agent does not do what he or she does *in order* to become unjust or intemperate; or, at least, that is a quite unusual case. But the agent does become unjust or intemperate voluntarily, and often can foresee or could have foreseen where a pattern of reaction, reasoning, and choice would or might lead.

People sometimes say things such as "Nobody back then thought that cocaine was addictive." Maybe so. And maybe there was little knowledge of the long-term health effects of heavy cocaine use. However, if one finds oneself in a more and more anxious pattern of increasing use of cocaine, that should be a signal of something important about dependence. This is quite different, for example, from not knowing that working with a certain material will cause damage (that manifests only long after exposure) to the health of those who are in regular contact with it. Or, maybe the agent doesn't mind the dependence on cocaine and is not worried by thoughts of remote effects. If she then goes on using it, her use of it is voluntary insofar as it is what she chooses to do, even if it is becoming more and more a matter of addiction. Similarly, the agent may not see that a pattern of activity is likely to establish a state of character but is capable of the sort of awareness that would enable her to judge whether it is desirable that that pattern should become second nature. Thoughts of that kind may not occur to the agent and may not be part of deliberate self-examination, but that does not defeat the voluntariness of the practice or of the state once habit entrenches it.

A person may give no more deliberative thought to making a nasty remark than he gives to coughing when something is caught in his throat, but the former is voluntary in a way that the latter is not. Maybe this person *never* gives thought to whether or not to make a nasty remark; he is a nasty person. He was raised by nasty people, and his children are being raised by him to be nasty. (Though he never has the thought "I want my kids to be nasty.") We then know, to a large extent, how he and his children came to be nasty. Agents *can* intend and act in order to alter or bring about certain dispositions. They do not *have to* intend them in order to be responsible for them. In doing this, that, and the other thing, on account of general policies and dispositions, the agent brings about an overall state of character even though there may not have been an enduring, explicit intention to bring about just *that* as the overall result. Perhaps it could have been foreseen; people *are* often advised, encouraged, or warned by friends and family members and the police about where they are headed as a consequence of their actions. Still, knowledge of the eventuality is not a condition of its being brought about voluntarily.

There are situations in which we really do not know of the probable effects of a habit or of a regular practice and should not be expected to. Maybe we have been deceived or misled. Often, though, the problem is not ignorance, but inattention or denial. Even without expert knowledge of physiology or psychology there are many sound commonsense judgments we are able to make about the advisability of many habits. If we attend to our patterns of motivation, deliberation, and action in ways that we are typically well able to, we can detect evidence of habit-formation and of the significance of that for character. That is a difference between the issue of responsibility with regard to states of character and responsibility for a particular action. In the former, there is the temporally extended opportunity to consider what one is doing and what difference it can make. There are many points at which consideration of one's acts and dispositions can make a difference to states of character.

Inattention or lack of awareness of the causal tendencies of one's actions is often not sufficient to defeat responsibility for the resulting dispositions. They may constitute something like a kind of negligence, rather than exculpating ignorance, on account of the voluntariness of the actions that lead to them. Similarly, when we act in ways that lead to good habits and characteristics we often do so without thinking that they will lead to them or that they should. That is, we may not be motivated by the thought that so acting will help us acquire virtues. Still, the possession of those virtues, if attained, is voluntary, even given due weight to temperament and other factors that enter the circumstances without our having chosen them. Of course, an agent does not become virtuous 'blindly,' by accident, as it were, even when becoming virtuous is not a general, self-conscious goal. The agent will have awareness of himself as a deliberating agent and as exercising his capacities for action in some ways rather than others voluntarily. The same is typically true of agents who acquire dispositions we cannot admire or which are vicious.

We should distinguish between cases in which the agent is habituated badly on account of bad influences, and cases in which the agent is not subject to bad influences, but acquires bad habits anyway. The *results* may look very much the same. However, in the former, the agent's range of opportunity, examples, and practical vision are narrow in a way that they are not in the latter. With respect to the former, we might say of the agent "It was to be expected," whereas with respect to the latter, we might say "How could this happen?" or "What went wrong?"[13] In both cases the agents may not recognize ethical considerations in the right way, and we may not be able to motivate them to see things differently. In one case the agent turned out badly, and in the other, the agent allowed himself to go wrong or even cultivated bad habits. Still, characteristics that one acquires by encouragement can involve voluntariness in the acquisition. Of course, no one is simply free to acquire just any characteristics, if by 'free' we mean complete independence from influence and habituation. Our judgment of the bad man who has cultivated his character may appropriately be harsher than our judgment of the man who is bad on account of bad influence; the latter had a more difficult task. Still, each does what he does voluntarily, and that is an important part of the explanation of the bad habits of each. We should be careful not to conclude from the fact that an agent was subject to powerful influences that he is less of a responsible agent.

What has emerged overall is that there is an important point to identifying the special role of habituation prior to rational maturity; but (1) habituation does not drive out voluntariness, and (2) there are rational habits, habits of agents who act on the basis of their own practical reasoning. Adults establish habits in themselves, for which they are responsible, even if they are irresponsible habits.

Williams's objection to Aristotle's view seemed to be driven by the question "How can there be responsibility for character, given the weight carried by habituation?" There is a different direction of concern in respect to habituation, this one driven by the question "How can an agent acquire the virtues and become the sort of person who voluntarily and responsibly acts well, without habituation?" This includes the ways in which one acts habitually as a result of one's own voluntary initiatives, the ways in which one habituates oneself. It is obvious that habituation can be done badly and thereby generate impediments to virtue and perfection. Still, in its *own* right it is not a process that shrinks or defeats responsibility for character. Whether habituation is ethically sound or not, it typically makes the individual a no less full-fledged agent, and an agent to whom it is appropriate to ascribe responsibility both for character and for action.

HABITUATION AND TEMPERAMENT

We need to say a bit more about the significance of temperament because that is another crucial factor in shaping character, and one over which an agent seems to have even less control or capacity to change. Trianosky criticizes the Aristotelian account of responsibility for character for failing to correctly acknowledge the role of temperament. He says, "Character is the product not only of voluntary action but also of the activity of temperament, along with upbringing, childhood experiences, social environment, peer expectations, and pure happenstance. And not only temperament but all of these things are not themselves the product of some exercise of agency, whether voluntary or nonvoluntary. Hence, no Aristotelian account of responsibility for character can succeed."[14] The reason for this is that "Although one's attitudes, emotions, reactive capacities, and skills are or can to some extent be developed by will, no effort of will, however sustained, is *sufficient* for their development."[15]

Basic features of temperament play a very important nonconscious, and nondeliberate role in setting one's "patterns of commitment."[16] Whether we are particularly passive, malleable individuals, or especially alert, self-motivated and discriminating ones depends, to a significant extent, on matters of temperament, and similarly with respect to characteristics such as being cold and calculating or warm and generous. Trianosky says, "People's characters may be prone to develop, change, and stabilize in different ways and to different degrees. That is to say, people are inclined to act, choose, commit, endorse, and so on in different ways and to different degrees. To *do* these things is always, of course, to act voluntarily. Yet even so, the degree to which, and the manner in which one is disposed to make these changes is itself *largely a nonvoluntary matter.*"[17]

The emphasis on temperament is an important counterweight to exaggerated claims on behalf of deliberate self-making with regard to character. However, my argument has been that there is a coherent, plausible extension of the voluntary to encompass the issue of 'uptake' of one's constitutional luck. The uptake need not be a matter of large-scale, self-conscious planning, though it still reflects a way in which one is responsible for character. While it would be most implausible to hold people responsible for their temperaments, it is plausible to ascribe to them responsibility for the actions and characteristics through which temperament is expressed in choices, judgments, and reactions. We cannot choose our temperaments, though there is voluntariness at work in what temperament counts for in acts, intentions, and responses. It is susceptible to regulation and management. Indeed, a good deal of the most important habituation we undergo concerns the ways in which we are encouraged and the ways we encourage ourselves to manage temperament. Dealing with our temperaments, even just knowing them and being honest about them, are among the most important kinds of voluntary undertakings.

For example, the gossip may work at disciplining himself to break the habit, and the defensive or edgy person may work at trying to be a bit less volatile. This kind of sensitivity may be part of the agent's temperament and not traceable in any clear way to specific experiences or circumstances. We cannot fault him for having the sensitivity, but we can fault him for not coming to grips with it or for letting it control him. This is a different kind of task from trying to be more conscientious in fulfilling responsibilities or trying to be more scrupulously honest. In both cases there is a concern about what sort of person to be, but in one the concern is with the management of a natural propensity, in the other it is with conceptions of value. There is a normative dimension to each, but they are different kinds of normative dimensions. The sorts of affect and motivational materials involved are different. So too, are the expectations and responses of other people. If I have a habit of being less than fully honest, I am liable to blame and loss of credibility, whereas if I have an oversensitive temperament, I may not be faulted in the same sorts of ways, though there are still grounds for criticism of me if I do not control my reactions. My temperament may be a mitigating condition, to some extent. At least it is a factor that helps others understand why I act the way I do, in a different way from the fact that I am say, dishonest. Temperament and habit dispose, and set limits on the materials out of which mature character is fashioned, but the architecture of mature character is largely shaped by voluntary activity. Granted, that activity *reflects* temperament, but it is also (more or less) *responsive* to guidance, direction, reprimand, and so forth, addressed to us by others, and addressed to us by ourselves.

This interpretation of voluntariness can acknowledge that responsibility is sometimes defeated not just with respect to individual actions but also with respect to a person's character overall. There are people who have innate compulsions or who are, by nature, impeded from acquiring dispositions to good action. What 'comes naturally' to such persons is much more than ordinarily resistant to good habituation (or perhaps any habituation) and they are unable to acquire virtuous second natures. Aristotle too recognized that some states are the result of disease or madness, and that they are "outside the limits of vice, just as bestiality is" (*NE* 1149a1). In addition, he makes reference in Book I to "anyone who is not deformed [in his capacity] for virtue" (*NE* 1099b19). Perhaps the child in the example of confinement described earlier is an instance of that. She did not begin with constitutional defects but was maimed for virtue by conditions over which she had no control and which she had no ability to understand.

Of course, most people are not precluded from exercising voluntariness over the formation of second nature, and most are free of compulsions and other kinds of large-scale, persistent, responsibility-defeating conditions. This does not mean, though, that people typically exercise a particularly high degree of self-conscious control over their states of character, and we should guard against exaggerating the extent to which they do. The argument that agents are responsible for their characters is not based on the claim that in a straightforward way agents *intentionally* cause their own characters. There is an important difference between that sort of view and the claim that agents have responsibility for character because *what agents voluntarily and intentionally do* strongly influences their characters. It is the latter that is emphasized here.

Thus, as noted above, the voluntariness of character does not depend upon the agent acting in certain ways *in order that* she should have a certain character (though to some extent, people do this). But the argument is not simply, "Since action is voluntary, character is voluntary, because action influences character." The argument is that action is voluntary in ways that shape character and that agents can recognize that how they act makes a difference to what characteristics they acquire and which of them become features of fixed character and can regulate the process.

Aristotle observes: "Actions and states, however, are not voluntary in the same way. For we are in control of actions from the origin to the end, when we know the particulars. With states, however, we are in control of the origin but do not know, any more than with sicknesses, what the cumulative effect of particular actions will be; none the less, since it was up to us to exercise a capacity either this way or another way, states are voluntary" (*NE* 1114b30–1115a4). We noted earlier that we do not know at exactly what point a regular manner of behavior or reaction becomes habitual and second nature any more than we can say which trip into the mine put someone over the threshold for lung cancer. We do know, though, that, typically, resistance weakens with repetition or rationalization and that acts and even motives that earlier one might have more critically considered, or been hesitant about, can come more naturally as dispositional momentum gathers in their direction.

Voluntariness is reflected not only in actions but in in reactions as well. Irwin's explication of Aristotle is helpful. "Even if I act without deliberation and premeditation on a sudden impulse of emotion or appetite, the origin may still be in my character and decision; for the presence or strength of my desire may be the result of the character and decisions I have formed. I may have deliberately cultivated this sort of impulse, or I may have failed to do what I could reasonably be expected to do to prevent its growth. If my voluntary actions are related in this way to my decision and character, their origin is in *me* in the relevant sense, and I am fairly held responsible for them, even though an animal would not be held responsible for its voluntary actions."[18] This makes sense, given the role of the sentiments and desires in motivation and with regard to the reasons for action. If you hear news of someone's undeserved suffering, and it pleases you on account of your jealousy of that person, it is appropriate to treat that response as voluntary. Similarly with resentment, admiration, gratitude, sycophancy, and so forth. These are passions, or involve passions, but they are also reflective of judgments and are susceptible to revision through our efforts to see things differently. In that way, voluntariness is displayed in the sorts of sentiments that are second nature to us and in our stances with respect to them. Suppose that upon discovery that you have accidentally thrown away the cherished love letters, your response is, "Well, I guess you won't be enjoying that little treasure any longer." That does not make your discarding them voluntary, but it both indicates something about your character that is relevant to how you might act, and it is a voluntary response based on those same valuations.

CHARACTER AND LIMITS

Although character constitutes limits on what one can and cannot do, the discussion of voluntariness shows that these are limits that are shaped in part by the voluntary actions that establish character. There are limits that are strengths, and limits that are weaknesses. Perhaps the agent simply does not consider doing base or cowardly things, and ethically dubious considerations just have no appeal to this person. There is of course the vicious counterpart to this. Some agents are hardened against compassion or give no weight to considerations of fairness, and so forth. Character, as much as opportunity, delimits the range of what one can do. There may be many things that in the circumstances are 'up to' us in an abstract sense, given the causal possibilities, though they go unnoticed, or considerations in favor of them have no motivational traction for us or they are dismissed. Many of our capacities and incapacities are due to our own voluntariness and are not enabling or constraining conditions with sources external to us. They are limits which, in important ways, we bring about and sustain. We are responsible for the actions that reflect them.

Addressing this, Williams writes: "We are subject to the model that what one can do sets the limits to deliberation, and that character is revealed by what one chooses within those limits, among the things that one can do. But character (of a person in the first instance; but related points apply to a group, or to a tradition) is equally revealed in the location of those limits, and in the very fact that one can determine, sometimes through deliberation itself, that one cannot do certain things, and must do others. Incapacities can not only set limits to character and provide conditions of it, but can also partly constitute its substance."[19] And, "What I recognize, when I conclude in deliberation that I cannot do a certain thing, is a certain incapacity of mine."[20] An individual's freedom of action is shaped by that person's history of voluntary activity as well as by circumstances and by features of the past over which the agent had no control. What one (in the sense of an abstract *anyone*) can do in a situation sets highly general boundaries, but what this or that particular agent recognizes as doable or acceptable depends a good deal on character.

Williams points out that we sometimes make important discoveries about our characters in the project of deliberating. We may find out what we have 'in' us, or what we are 'made of,' what we 'must' do, or what we care about most deeply. That is not to say that we simply discover something about ourselves for which we are not responsible or over which we have no control. The deliberative project itself is an exercise of voluntariness, and how we regard and respond to what we find are also voluntary undertakings. They both reflect and partially constitute character. He says: "The context, nevertheless, [of making the discovery about oneself that one must do a certain thing] is one of practical reasoning, and that fact, together with the consideration that the incapacities in question are, in a broad sense, incapacities of character, will help to explain the important fact that this kind of incapacity cannot turn away blame."[21] This issue will be of special significance in the discussion of ethical disability in chapter 2.

A limitation may be a limitation on how one deliberates about what to do, or it may be a limitation on the ways in which one responds to situations and other people. We might criticize someone, saying, "Couldn't you see that doing that was unfair and hurtful? Couldn't you see that doing that would aggravate an already unhappy and difficult situation?" And the response might be "Oh, shut up; I can't be bothered with worrying about other people's feelings." This response might be quite sincere, not just bravado masking guilt or insecurity. This agent's limitations do not yield an excusing condition any more than the virtuous agent's inability to participate in a fraud or to knowingly blame the innocent defeats responsibility.

Consider the various different senses of the expression "I have to . . . ." It sometimes means that one very much *wants* to, as in "I have to try that new restaurant." Or, "I have to" might mean that not to do the thing would be a violation of a rule, as in 'I have to move my piece; the game requires it"; or, "I have to renew my motor vehicle registration." It can also mean that this is what I have to do instrumentally, in order to meet a need, or satisfy a desire; e.g., "I have to get someone to show me how to fix that dishwasher," or "I have to practice my French if I am going on that trip." It can also mean that to do the thing meets a moral requirement that I am honoring, as in "I made that promise in good faith, and I have to keep it." 'Have to' can also be a matter of a requirement of etiquette. For example, if you are to attend a formal dinner, you have to wear shoes and socks. Or, you have to have refreshments for guests who have arrived after a long and arduous journey. There is also the 'have to' of limited alternatives, as in the case where you have to go down the unreliable fire escape because the other exits are blocked by smoke and fire.

There is, though, another type of 'have to' and it is explicated in terms of the agent's character. Williams speaks of a 'must' which is grounded in character or a discovery about character, and it is much the same thing that I am referring to here. He says, "To arrive at a conclusion that one must do a certain thing is, typically, to make a discovery—a discovery which is, always minimally and sometimes substantially, a discovery about oneself."[22] There may be things one has to do, not because of causal determinants or in order to satisfy some specific requirement, but as a matter of being who one is, or finding out who one is. Whatever the risks, legality, or other conditions relevant to the issue of what you do when the fugitive slave seeks refuge at your house, how you address the situation may be a matter of what you have to do in this last sense. What you do may not flow straightforwardly from your character. The situation may be such that facing it (or even the decision to face it) involves making discoveries about your own character.

You might have the thought that you have to do whatever you can to help that person, and, in having that thought, perhaps you make a discovery about your convictions, your courage, and what you, in the actual event, are willing to risk. Or, quite differently, you might have the thought that it is something of a privilege to have a desperate person at your mercy, and you relish condemning this individual to a miserable fate. There is no dilemma or conflict for you. In such cases we can plausibly speak, as Williams does, of "practical necessity" without this indicating diminished voluntariness or diminished responsibility. Williams's discussion of practical necessity indicates ways in which our conceptions of different kinds of practical impossibility and necessity are to be understood, in large part, by examining character, and not exclusively or mainly through a consideration of the causal possibilities that circumstances present.

In the final portion of his discussion he writes, "Conclusions of practical necessity seriously arrived at in serious matters are indeed the paradigm of what one takes responsibility for."[23] I would add that there are conclusions concerning practical necessity which are not arrived at by careful thought and that agents are responsible for those as well, because of how they are reflective of character. Temperament is important here, because of how it shapes features of the motivational and deliberative terrain. Still, how we move about on that terrain and what directions we move in are matters for which we are responsible. That some things go unacknowledged as possibilities by our deliberations and that some sorts of motives never have any energy for us is often indicative of the fixity of character or at least firm resolutions of self-determination, rather than being indicative of voluntariness shrunken by circumstances or by external forces.[24]

It could be objected that maybe *mature* agents can reason about policies of action and select ends and projects, but all of that activity is undertaken by a character *already* formed, over which the agent had very little control. Thus, the account may seem problematic in the following way: It holds that we are most responsible for our characters and the actions that flow from them at that time in life when character is most fixed and least susceptible to revision. But, earlier, when there is the *most* plasticity in our characters, and they are being formed, we are least able to exercise control over what dispositions we acquire because we are not yet critical, experience-informed practical reasoners. How can those claims be reconciled? How *can* we be responsible for our characters?

There is a distinction we noted earlier that helps in responding to this objection. A person can have beliefs, values, motivational tendencies, and so forth, that is, characteristics, without those constituting a stable, established character. As a person matures, it is reasonable to expect more capacity for practical reasoning and evaluation of one's ends and motives, and more awareness of the influence of one's own actions on character. One is better able to see that what one does and the ways in which one is motivated make a difference to what sort of character is settled into. The account acknowledges the number and variety of influences at work in forming character. However, that formation is taking place in an agent who is increasingly able to make his own judgments, acknowledge his responsibility for his acts and their outcomes, and to consider and revise his motives and aims. There is no time during which the individual does not have characteristics, though there is a role for voluntariness with respect to the formation and content of mature character.

BEING RESPONSIBLE AND TAKING RESPONSIBILITY

An agent can also be responsible for features of his character that he does not reflectively endorse and with which he does *not* identify. There are ways of being responsible for a characteristic even though one does not *take* responsibility for it. Perhaps it is a characteristic that reflects a natural disposition that could be modified by habit; perhaps it is formed in large part by the agent's pattern of voluntary activity. Perhaps there were opportunities for changing this characteristic, but the agent has "continually passed up any such opportunities for improvement—just out of a kind of inertia, rather than a project of building or maintaining a certain sort of character; and not, on the other hand, because it would have been particularly difficult to do otherwise."[25] This too, is a kind of habituation. It is, as it were, habituation by neglect. It is leaving alone a disposition that one might have considered and undertaken to alter. The result may be a characteristic which is difficult to change, but for which the agent is responsible, even though there was no deliberate policy of cultivating it and no policy of self-conscious identification with it.

On the other hand, an agent might take a certain kind of responsibility for dispositions that plainly are *not* the result of voluntary activity. This is not a matter of thinking of oneself as the cause of the disposition but acknowledging that this disposition is a feature or part of one's character. Recall the example of being oversensitive or edgy. Acknowledging a constitutive feature of one's character can reflect and also promote certain important kinds of self-knowledge, for example, knowledge of one's temperament. Sometimes we acknowledge motives or passions that we are susceptible to and see those as part of our make-up but we do not endorse them and would rather be free of them than fully identify with them. This acknowledgment can be part of an effort to control, moderate, or inhibit them. Suppose, for example, that the agent is someone who is easily angered. He might recognize this and take responsibility for it in the respect that he knows that this is something about himself that he should manage better or try to overcome. In that kind of case, the agent is not taking responsibility for bringing about the disposition but for how it figures in his motives and actions and for the attempt to modify it. When he feels or displays anger in ways in which he wishes he did not, he sees doing so as his own act, and that is why he gets so upset with himself over it. In such cases, our motives are not lined up with our values in the way that we wish them to be, but the acts are still voluntary, and we are still responsible. The agent may wonder "Why do I do these things?" as though he were being compelled by something, but this may also be a way of confronting oneself with the realization that acting in that way can be responsive to voluntary efforts at control.

In many cases, to say that a person's actions are determined by the person's character is all right, as long as we recognize that this is not the same as saying that there are no respects in which action and character are voluntary. (And we acknowledge that discoveries about one's own character, achieved *in* deliberating, are also possible.) There are certain things that he *of course* does, and there are certain ways of seeing things that are *of course* his ways of seeing them. We should not, however, conclude on those grounds alone that the agent is any less a voluntary or responsible agent. At an early age the 'of course' is the 'of course' of nature, of temperament. The individual is not yet thinking about what to do in terms of reasons. Later on, when we note that the agent did what was to be expected, given who he is, that refers to his voluntarily acquired second nature and his policies of practical reasoning.

We need to see habit as having as much texture as voluntariness, and we need to see the ways in which they can be mutually supportive rather than exclusive. This will bring into view the substantial respect in which we are typically responsible for our characters, even though we exercise our agency in settings (and from capacities) that are fraught with luck. Being self-centered or squeamish may be just be part of who you are but such characteristics are susceptible to voluntary control. An agent can be expected to acknowledge that he has a disposition that needs to be addressed by his own attention and that it can make a difference to address it. Not to do so would be an ethical fault, an appropriate ground for criticism (even if not deep or grave criticism) because of what we can reasonably expect people to undertake voluntarily by way of habituating themselves.

The discussion so far has been preliminary to an explication of ethical disability. We will see that there are certain ways of becoming ethically disabled that do not defeat responsibility. Habituation, both by others and by oneself, and one's history of voluntary activity can lead to a condition in which the agent's appreciation of good and patterns of motivation are fixed in wrong or perverse ways. The agent may act on conceptions of value that appear good to him but are in fact not good, and the agent does not regret acting on them. Nor does he have an effective capacity to correct his conceptions and his dispositions. This is a person who, by his own voluntary activity, has become ethically disabled.

CHAPTER 2

Ethical Disability and Responsibility

Some agents develop characters that disable them for sound ethical comprehension and action. The agent whose vices are especially persistent and entrenched, to the extent that she cannot appreciate ethical considerations in a correct manner, is *ethically disabled.*[1] I shall argue that there are such agents, of whom it is not true that 'ought' implies 'can.' The adjustments we would have to make in order to either explain away ethical disability or to diminish the responsibility of ethically disabled agents are less plausible than the considerations that enable us to recognize the reality of ethical disability.

There are agents who are ethically disabled through no fault of their own and of course, when the disability is not voluntary, that does defeat responsibility. Examples are agents who are insane or delusional or afflicted with compulsive disorders. These are states that drive motivation or that influence or destroy judgment *no matter what.* Also, there are people who are mentally handicapped or who as a result of injury or dementia have significantly limited or reduced cognitive and practical capacity. The disabling may also be the result of particularly vicious maltreatment. (Recall the example of the little girl who was confined for years.) Agents suffering from these are not the ethically disabled agents of concern right here. Our main concern is whether there are agents who are both disabled and responsible. Both types of agents may be resistant to change, but that is not the decisive issue. There is a historical dimension to the ethical disability of agents who remain responsible. Of course, one can come to be nonresponsibly disabled because of natural or social history. But the weight of emphasis in the relevant cases is on the agent's own history of voluntary activity. The agents at issue are capable of practical reasoning, and they knowingly enact values that they endorse. It is their history as voluntary agents that explains their state of disability.

There might be reason to regard at least the amoralist as ethically disabled. There are agents whose amoralism is not pathological, but a deliberate undertaking and the responsibility of those agents is not defeated. Such agents may understand that certain kinds of valuative concern weigh heavily with others but those concerns just do not matter to these agents. The amoralist is not an agent who cares about nothing or who has no valuative commitments, yet he rejects what in fact are true ethical values and resolutely refuses to make them attachments that guide him in his life. This agent may be rational and responsible in the most general sense of being an agent in control of what he does, even if we appropriately regard him as somewhat menacing or disturbing. Given his self-conception and commitments he may develop a character that puts sound ethical cognition out of his reach. But his defects are ethical defects, not defects that lessen his status as a responsible agent.

We should distinguish the ethically disabled agent from the agent who is basically decent but who sometimes acts badly, and also from the agent who has vices, perhaps even quite serious ones, but who also recognizes them and has some genuine interest in overcoming them. The ethically disabled agent who has been disabled by voluntary activity is more fully cut-off from sound ethical requirements both judgmentally and motivationally. This is why even rational appeals to this agent have little prospect of success. However, this is not someone whose responsibility is lessened on account of her lack of understanding.

ACCESSIBILITY AND DISABILITY

One reason for reluctance to regard ethically disabled agents as responsible is that we often interpret unethical behavior as a lapse. The religious tradition has had a significant influence here, through the idea of fallenness, but the notion of acting badly as involving lapse has a standing without theological presuppositions. We typically regard ethical failures as failures to uphold standards grounded in principles or criteria that are (at least to some extent) understood and acknowledged by the agents who have acted badly. That is a sense in which many people suppose that every otherwise normal agent is ethically capable. But not everyone *is* ethically capable. Not every agent is able to correctly appreciate ethical considerations in the way needed to support that supposition. Sometimes when people act badly it is not because they flout or violate norms or criteria that they recognize, but because they are doing what they take to be perfectly all right, though it is in fact wrong, and they cannot understand the wrongness of their values.

When we find that agents are not responsive to rational appeals concerning their values, ends, and motives, that often seems to give us reason to doubt whether they merit the full measure of responsibility. We find it difficult to recognize seriously vicious people as full-fledged rational agents. In response, we reinterpret their vice as flowing from a nonvoluntary condition that has degraded their capacity as rational agents. The incorrigible agent seems to be pathological rather than voluntarily awful. Sometimes that indeed is the case. Sometimes it is not.

The idea that ethical considerations are accessible in a basically unproblematic way is found, for example, in Kant's moral philosophy and also in Mill's. For all of the differences between them, there is this point of contact: namely, there is a fundamental criterion of moral judgment and it is accessible to all. (I realize that Kant and Mill were talking about distinctively moral judgment, and not ethics in the broader sense I indicated in the Introduction. Still, their accounts of the accessibility of the criteria of moral judgment are apt for the present discussion.) Kant took his account of the fundamental principle of morality to be an account of something already at work in the plain person's practical reason, even if the philosophical explication and justification of it belong to the metaphysics of morals. It was important to him that the categorical imperative should be recognized as the principle of *common* moral knowledge. He remarks that "within the moral knowledge of common human reason we have attained its principle."[2] He notes that "the most remarkable thing about ordinary reason in its practical concern is that it may have as much hope as any philosopher of hitting the mark. In fact, it is almost more certain to do so than the philosopher, because he has no principle which the common understanding lacks, while his judgment is easily confused by a mass of irrelevant considerations, so that it easily turns aside from the correct way."[3] He does not intend the principle that he identifies to reflect a revision of morality, and he insists that at least at the level of first-order morality it is safe to "acquiesce in the common rational judgment."[4] For his part, Mill thought the ethical significance of utility was already widely taken into account in any plausible moral view (indeed, that it would be very strange and implausible if it were not) and that the doctrine of utility "does supply, if not always an easy, at all events a tangible and intelligible, mode"[5] of deciding differences on moral questions. He also held that there is no special difficulty in recognizing the truth of the doctrine. No special theoretical knowledge is needed.

In holding that the principle of moral requirement, or moral requirements themselves are generally accessible, Kant and Mill represent an important current of thought about morality; namely, that we are united in a common moral world not only by each having equal moral status, but by each having the ability to recognize the criterion of right action and the ability to apply it.[6] We are all, in a sense, equally morally capable because we can each comprehend true value. There is, in a broad sense, an egalitarian democracy of both moral status and ability. I do not mean that they (and other theorists) made no allowance for the role of character and personal history, but that an important element of many of the most influential moral theories is that any agent who is sane and rational is thereby able to recognize and appreciate ethical considerations.

But this is not true. Some people, as a result of habituation and their own voluntary activity are rendered less able to recognize and appreciate the considerations that figure in sound ethical judgment. It is on that basis that we are able to understand how a good deal of vicious activity is *not* to be interpreted as a lapse, but rather, as a 'success' at something else, viz., pursuit of the agent's wrong values. There are agents who are largely insulated against ethically appropriate guilt and shame, who are unmoved to reconsider their acts, and are unmoved by what is in fact apt criticism of them. This is not because these agents are intrinsically bad but because their practical reason is disordered in a way which is an obstacle to their recognizing the defects in their valuative conceptions.

The responsible disabled agent has wrong or perverse values but is not so unlike the rest of us that he is not recognizably a participant in an ethical world he shares with us. Granted, the agent who becomes ethically disabled as a result of his own voluntary activities is not someone who acts under descriptions that register that acting that way may be ethically disabling. He does not intend to incapacitate himself, though he may, for example, intend to humiliate certain people or deliberately teach his children to hate them. Those intentions reflect and reinforce his state but he does not think of them as vicious intentions. His actions have the effect of disabling him, and once these states of character are fixed, his capacity to judge well and to be virtuously motivated may be seriously diminished. The rational appeal of sound ethical considerations will have greatly reduced resonance for this person, and indeed, may not even be heard, though this is not someone who is congenitally 'deaf' to ethical considerations.

McDowell's use of the notion of 'silencing' can help explicate this. He has argued that a difference between a virtuous individual and one who lacks virtue is that in the virtuous person's view of a situation, considerations which have motivational influence for the weak or vicious person are "silenced by the recognized requirement."[7] In explicating the difference between temperance and continence, McDowell says that the temperate agent "need be no less prone to enjoy physical pleasure than the next man."[8] However, given the way he appreciates situations, "his clear perception of the requirement insulates the prospective enjoyment—of which, for a satisfying conception of the virtue, we should want him to have a vivid appreciation—from engaging his inclinations at all. Here and now, it does not count for him as any reason for acting that way."[9] This, he acknowledges, is an ideal, but the point is that different things count to the virtuous agent and the vicious agent, rather than just the same things counting, but in different ways.

McDowell argues that "It would be wrong to infer that the conceptions of situations which constitute the reasons are available equally to people who are not swayed by them, and weigh with those who are swayed only contingently upon their possession of an independent desire. . . . We should say that the relevant conceptions are not so much as possessed except by those whose wills are influenced appropriately."[10] For the virtuous agent what is silenced is not first considered, then found uncompelling, and then dismissed or driven out. It does not occur as a motivating consideration. For example, an agent may have a character such that the possibility of covering up an error or oversight of his own by blaming someone else (who happens not to be in a position to defend herself) just does not arise. If it were suggested to the agent to do so, it would be immediately rejected instead of first being thought about and tested for practicability and then outweighed or found to involve too much risk.

We should add that silencing is not peculiar to virtue. It has to do with how firmly established are the agent's characteristics and how effectively they limit what the agent takes to be action-guiding considerations. Thus, it can be a feature of vice as well as of virtue. The agent with a cold willingness to make others suffer, or the agent who takes pleasure in the degradation and suffering of others because of his contempt or loathing for them is someone for whom various considerations that would count heavily for the decent person go unheard. The vicious agent enjoys the wrong things and his endorsement of the pleasure he takes in them may not be disrupted or distracted by a background acknowledgment that they are wrong and may not be challenged by remorse. For this sort of agent, the willingness to cause suffering, to be unjust, to be unresponsive to dire need, and so forth, are not registered as lapses and are not to be explained by the interference of passion or appetite. The willingness is reflective of the agent's values.

We can clarify ethical disability a bit more by distinguishing the ethically disabled agent from the vicious agent as described by Aristotle. He says of vicious agents that "they are at odds with themselves, and, like incontinent people, have an appetite for one thing and a wish for another" (*NE* 1166b7–8). Also, "Those who have done many terrible actions hate and shun life because of their vice, and destroy themselves" (*NE* 1166b12–13). He says of the vicious agent, "his soul is in conflict, and because he is vicious one part is distressed at being restrained, and another is pleased [by the intended action]; and so each part pulls in a different direction, as though they were tearing him apart. Even if he cannot be distressed and pleased at the same time, still he is soon distressed because he was pleased, and wishes these things had not become pleasant to him; for base people are full of regret" (*NE* 1166b20–25). This characterization of the internal conflict and instability that wrack the soul does seem apt with respect to many agents. There are, though, other vicious agents who are still rational but who are not disturbed in these ways, not subject to the disruption that we might expect (or, in certain moods, hope) to encounter as a penalty for vice. Those are ethically disabled agents. I see no reason why vice cannot silence and leave the agent quite undisturbed. The pursuit of immoral ends may make it impossible for the vicious agent to love himself in the way that the virtuous agent does. But it will not inevitably cause him to be discomfited in a way that will supply reasons to act and judge differently that are recognized by the agent. The vicious agent who has no conception of virtuous self-love may not miss what he cannot have. As we noted earlier, this is not an agent who is mentally ill, nor is this an agent who is overcome by desire or passion in an episodic way, an agent who has temporarily lost control. Ethical disability involves endorsement of the values enacted even if the agent cannot be bothered with moral values; his concerns lie entirely elsewhere. There is more to this than abnormal sensibility, and the 'more' concerns the agent's conception of what counts as reasons worth enacting.

Kant says of even "the most malicious villain"[11] that so long as he is accustomed to using his reason he "wishes to be free from such inclinations"[12] which move him to act badly, and that he regards them as "burdensome even to himself."[13] He too, would wish to have such qualities as "honesty of purpose, of steadfastness in following good maxims, and of sympathy and general benevolence even with sacrifice of advantages and comfort . . ."[14] when examples of excellence are presented to him. In Kant's view, as long as one has not lost or abandoned reason altogether, it is possible to think of oneself as a moral legislator and it is possible to take an interest in the moral law because of its validity. The possession of reason will enable an agent to recognize both the fact that, and the way in which, moral requirements have gone unmet. Moreover, respect for one's own reason will enable the agent to morally retrieve himself.

The Kantian view clearly expresses the widely shared supposition that immoral action is a lapse from an available standard. We often ask others, "How could you not know that that was wrong?" or, "How could you not see how unfair, or cruel it was to do that?" We ask ourselves, "What did I think I was doing?" We typically reprimand and judge on the basis of an assumption that there is a substantial moral minimum grasped by anyone who is not mentally defective or cognitively handicapped. We shall see that this assumption is optimistic beyond the grounds given or assumed in support of it, and also that on Kant's view there is a capacity for something like rationalistic grace. Some theories of conscience (a topic we will take up in chapter 4) fulfill a similar function. Conscience is often thought to be a resource for ethical guidance that is present in each rational, sane agent, and it is thought to have a distinctive bindingness. It is thought that either an appeal to conscience can restore the agent's moral compass, or at least conscience will exact a price, in the form of remorse and self-reproach, that can only go unpaid by a substantial effort of self-deception.

Yet, aren't there people whose moral comprehension is so disordered that in acting badly they are not being inattentive to, or lapsing from, criteria or standards that in some sense they understand? They see themselves as being true to other values. When they act wrongly they do not feel the need to rationalize because they are acting on what they take to be good reasons, and they would be uninterested in, or scornful of, what are indeed correct considerations. This is not because ethically disabled agents lack some basic capacity but because their capacities have been exercised in ways that have fixed them in corrupt dispositions. What distinguishes the ethically disabled agent is that his grasp and appreciation of ethical matters is seriously and persistently defective. He may even achieve some partial recognition of the relevant considerations but he does not take them to be reasons that motivate him. It is not important to him to enact those values. This is the agent who does not understand his ethical defects *as* defects. He does not feel shame or remorse over (what is in fact) his misperception of the values in question or his lack of concern to enact them and his willingness to act for other kinds of reasons.

THE DIFFICULTY OF OVERCOMING ETHICAL DISABILITY

For those whose virtues silence various considerations there may be no strategy of argument that would get them to change their minds and their ways. There may be strategies of threat that would get them to act in certain ways, but threat is not argument. Some ways of seeing situations will be impossible for them because of their character. They will be very nearly incapacitated for evil. Given their dispositions and modes of perceiving, they could not do otherwise. The counterpart to this is the virtuous agent's inability to see any appeal at all in the considerations that are action-guiding for the vicious agent. There is a symmetry here that is inadequately acknowledged if we take wrongdoing always to be a lapse. Indeed, the vicious person may be quite nearly uncomprehending when the wrongfulness of his acts is explained to him. That, obviously, is a significant impediment to any sort of repentance or reform which is more than merely superficial and prudential. Perhaps the agent can be convinced on prudential grounds to alter his behavior in certain ways, but neither should we insist on that as a necessary condition for the agent's rationality. Maybe this person is strongly enough committed to his wrong values to remain true to them and explicitly reject or despise what in fact are true values.

Even in the case in which he is able to come to some sort of acknowledgment of his vices, the agent may be unable to effectively change in the direction of virtue. Sarah Broadie writes: "Now if the vicious person comes to hate himself and his modes of practical acceptance, it does not follow that he knows in a practical way how else to be or even how to begin to change. At the moments of choice and action he has no other moves to make, and no other ways of seeing and classifying his particular circumstances, than those which express the detested character."[15] He may have some understanding of the values that condemn his action or character, but they are not his values and he is unable to fully make them his own in a course of ethical self-correction. He may even want to, but the momentum of mature dispositions is hard to alter and, as Broadie's remarks suggest, part of what can be so painful and confusing to the agent is that he does not know how to go about actually making the changes. A young person who has been habituated badly is in a comparable situation in some ways, though there is still plasticity in his character. We may see that he is headed in a bad direction though there is time for him to change. The adult may not be able to change or overcome his established second nature, even with a measure of comprehension of what his second nature should be.

Ethical disability, like virtue, is a matter of degree, and I do not want to claim that there are voluntarily ethically disabled agents who categorically *cannot*, as a matter of conceptual impossibility, change their understanding and dispositions in the direction of virtue. Moreover, we would be epistemically overconfident if we claimed that we could reliably ascertain just who is ethically disabled. People (like our gossip in chapter one) sometimes do successfully undertake a process of changing a characteristic, and this can make for wider and enduring positive changes. It shows that at least some characteristics are not yet fully fixed. At the same time we should acknowledge that often it is unreasonable to expect a person to overcome defects of judgment and character or to be motivated to do so. The agent's dispositions may be firm to the extent that his habits and actions are aligned against the likelihood of change for the better. Or, the agent at some level might achieve some accurate recognition of the ethical character of his actions, but still be overwhelmingly motivated to persist in vicious habits without regret that disturbs him. (The notorious bank robber John Dillinger once wrote a letter to be published in a newspaper, discouraging young boys from regarding him as a hero and from emulating him. For his own part, he did not stop robbing banks and hurting people in the process.)

In addition, we should not in general expect teaching and argument to overcome what habit has established. Those who are firmly established in vice are of course less likely to be responsive to ethical arguments and appeals, and justifications of what are correct ethical views may be unavailing with them. "What argument could reform people like these [those who 'have not even a notion of what is fine']? For it is impossible, or not easy, to alter by argument what has long been absorbed by habit" (*NE* 1179b17–18). This is not because they are in the grip of a responsibility-defeating condition. They are in control of what they do, though quite limited with regard to the extent to which they can do otherwise. They are not irrational and they can coherently assign weight to considerations and make judgments and decisions on the basis of those assignments. They fail to be responsive to reason in the sense that how things *count* for them disagrees with correct understanding.

Perhaps the agent's way of seeing things is what is culturally or socially transmitted, as is the case with various forms of bigotry and xenophobia. (More on this issue follows.) Or, someone might regard the willingness to commit violent or harmful acts as a mark of courage, or may regard self-restraint in the satisfaction of appetites as a kind of timidity, indicative of weakness. Even if under critical scrutiny these views fall apart as soon as they are tested, the point is that people who have such views probably do not critically scrutinize them or feel any need to and may be sure of themselves in their mistaken ways. The way *they* see it, intimidation of members of certain groups is laudable, or it is all right to be very selective about honesty. They may genuinely believe that certain others are not owed the truth and the respect of being dealt with honestly. On the part of the dishonest agents, there may be no recognition of a double standard. The way they see it, it is not a matter of "I know I should not do this, but I am going to anyway." Rather, it is a matter of "This is what I think good, so this is what I am going to do."

It would be a mistake to interpret the case of the ethically disabled agent as a matter of what his reason is telling him running up against motivational obstacles rooted in his appetites and passions. His disability is a matter of *what his reason tells him*. That is what is so difficult for us to be reconciled to, and the difficulty reflects the notion that wrongdoing is a lapse. Namely, there is in the background the assumption that we each have in us the capacity, some resource for moral recognition, for moral retrieval of ourselves if we are not insane. We find it hard to understand how someone who in a basic respect is cognitively and rationally competent could nevertheless be unresponsive to, or scornful of, what right reason says. This is difficult to understand, but, of course, reason doesn't 'say it' to him.

It is true that because we have rational capacities we are able to make adjustments in our ethical beliefs and are able to fashion new policies of action. Without reason there could be no voluntary revision of practical policies and dispositions. That however, does not imply that reason can always be efficacious in bringing about such changes in the right direction. It is plain that in respect of practical reason, how one *has* exercised reason makes a difference to how one *can* do so. Ethically relevant characteristics do eventually constitute settled character, and firmly established bad habits of reasoning and judgment can seriously corrupt the capacity for ethically sound practical reasoning. Recalling the discussion of practical necessity and the way in which character can shape what one 'has to' or cannot do, we should say that these can be just as practically binding for the bad agent as for the good one. If he is firmly fixed in these habits, we should not expect him, though he is rational, to acknowledge the proper weight of ethical considerations. Yet, given his understanding of value, he does not perceive that anything is amiss on his part. Why not judge this agent to be less than fully rational, if rationality is more than formal rationality? He does not have correct understanding and he makes profound and persistent errors with regard to value. Why aren't those failures of rationality that amount to irrationality? The main reason is that the agent is no less a voluntary agent enacting his own practical reasoning. The quality of his reasoning is poor because of error, ignorance, attention, and other factors. But its poor quality does not disqualify him as a rational agent apt for the relevant sorts of attributions, assessments, and liabilities.

If one is lucky and has been habituated by virtuous people, or at least by decent people and also lives in a social world shaped by basically sound values, then plainly the chances of acquiring the virtues are much increased. However, bad luck in that respect is not automatically a condition for a corresponding diminution of responsibility. This might seem obnoxiously unfair, as though an unlucky individual thereby has bad luck aggravated by harsh judgment. This reaction is indicative of a way in which some real stress can be put on this claim of symmetry. We need to examine where the stress comes from and whether the view can carry it or deflect it.

The view we are developing is opposed to the view elaborated by Susan Wolf. She argues that "an individual is responsible if and only if she is able to form her actions on the basis of her values *and* she is able to form her values on the basis of what is True and Good."[16] In support of this, she writes: "A victim of a deprived (or depraved) childhood, for example, may be as smart as a person raised in a more normal environment, but, because of a regrettably skewed set of experiences, her values may be distorted. She is able to reason, as it were, but not able to act in accordance with Reason. Having been exposed to an unfortuitous collection of data, *her* reason will not reach its goal."[17]

She asks us to:

Consider the ordinary citizen living in Germany in the 1930s, the white child brought up on a southern plantation in the 1850s, or anyone brought up forty years ago to become a "lady" or a "gentleman" and to accept conventional sex roles as deep features of human nature or civilized society. Although it would be difficult to establish, even in individual cases, that such people were unable to see and appreciate the injustice of some of the practices, attitudes, and institutions of their communities, insofar as we do regard social processes and norms as potential obstacles to sound moral judgments, we lessen the blame we would otherwise direct toward individuals who, surrounded by these obstacles, fail to reach these judgments.[18]

The plausibility of Wolf's view is supported by an acknowledgment many would indeed wish to make; that is, if a certain way of seeing things is not available to an agent, we cannot blame the agent for not seeing things in that way. It would be unrealistic to expect just anybody, whatever their background and circumstances, to be able to see things in accord with right reason and to act as genuine virtue requires. Recognizing the role of habituation and the power of the prevailing norms makes that clear. Capacities for practical rationality are developed in settings strongly shaped by one's overall surroundings and more 'local' circumstances and predicaments and cannot be developed or exercised in abstraction from them. (We should note, for example, that while the present account relies heavily on Aristotelian resources, there are significant elements of Aristotle's own normative commitments which, with good reason, we find seriously mistaken. Given his time and circumstances, we can understand why he held those views. We can also ask whether those conditions are in some way responsibility-diminishing for an agent whose life was conditioned by them. It is not obvious what is the correct answer.) Prevailing conditions make an important difference to agents' ethical outlook and commitments. In addition, large scale, shared changes of values and perspectives in the direction of virtue can take a very long time, as social attitudes and prevailing perspectives tend to change slowly (and not always for the better).

The key point, however, is that even if there is a good deal that stands in the way of people engaging with true values, they are typically responsible for engaging with the values with which they engage. If I am correct about the substantial role of voluntariness in the development of character and the endorsement of values, there are grounds for substantial attributions of responsibility to mature agents even when the range of their valuative options is narrow and there are epistemic limits on access. Good luck in epistemic position can help one get things right, but is not a condition of responsibility for the values that are partially constitutive of character.

Addressing Wolf's view, Michele Moody-Adams writes: "The alleged victims of misguided societies seem to have actively feared and avoided self-reflection [*sic*] of the likelihood that it would undermine the contested values. Victims of abusive or deprived childhoods, in contrast, seem to fear and avoid self-reflection because it tends to intensify awareness of profoundly unhappy or desperate circumstances. Wolf is right to call attention to the lack of self-reflection in these cases, but in neither case can she show that such people lack the fundamental human capacity for self-reflection and self-correction."[19] Moody-Adams says this by way of arguing that Wolf has implausibly overstated the role of luck with regard to the abilities by virtue of which one is a responsible agent. This is part of her view that character is not destiny; that people typically retain the ability to revise their characters. With the respect to the first matter, we can agree with Moody-Adams. There is a role for the agent which Wolf has underestimated or argued out of existence on account of the state of the agent which eventuates. With respect to the second matter, I think it is implausibly optimistic to hold that the *effective* ability to change character is something people *typically* retain. We should continue to attribute responsibility for character to agents even if their capacity for self-correction is less robust than Moody-Adams suggests. (This will be discussed further in chapter 3.) She is surely correct to point out the different motivations for unwillingness to engage in self-reflection. My point is that that unwillingness (of many types, for a variety of reasons) combined with the way in which habits become second nature, can effectively undermine the capacity for genuine self-correction, even though when that is the case, it does not automatically diminish responsibility.

It would be implausible to insist that an agent is not responsible except when in an epistemic position to get moral values right. Again, this may sound punitive and in gross violation of the principle that one should be obligated only to do what one can do. Nevertheless, if there were not considerations supporting the interpretation of action as responsible independent of facts about the agent's being positioned to acquire ethical knowledge, we would often have to withhold ascriptions of responsibility from agents who know what they are doing, who are enacting values that they endorse, and who are acting voluntarily. The fact that their values are perverse, or that they have acquired them through a generations-long process of social custom and teaching, does not make them less responsible for the normative dimensions of their acts and the rationales that they accept for them.

When a society sustains wrong or perverse values this invites an attempt to understand why it has those values and how people who endorse them might be reachable in respect to achieving a better normative understanding. Our interest, or the interest of a courageous internal reformer, might focus on how constructive change might be brought about rather than simply on blame. But that does not mean that the responsibility of members of that society is diminished. The measure of understanding that we acquire does not displace an equal measure of the agent's responsibility.

I am not making a case for something like a blanket ethical 'strict liability.' The key disagreement with Wolf's view is the claim that it is an error to make the inference from the pervasiveness of ethical corruption and its power in shaping the normative horizon to the conclusion that there is diminished responsibility. Those matters can, and indeed should, be somewhat prised apart. Otherwise, we will find that we are misrepresenting and misjudging vast amounts of unethical behavior and wrongdoing undertaken by rational agents and making responsibility beholden to luck to an implausibly extensive degree. Ethical responsibility is more a matter of whether the agent is responsible for acts that are ethically relevant than a matter of whether the agent is or is in a position to become a virtuous agent.

ABILITY, CHARACTER, AND RESPONSIBILITY

The ethically disabled individual we are describing is a full-fledged practical reasoner, but he exercises the relevant capacities in ethically disordered ways. It is true that his understanding of good is not the understanding that right reason endorses and that he acts on ethically counterfeit or specious imperatives. We might be led to the conclusion that the agent is less than rational if we insist that the criterion of right reason is, as Kant held it to be, *the* law of practical reason itself. However, the agent's failure to correctly recognize and appreciate ethical considerations may be attributable to his own voluntary policies of judgment and motivation; that is, to his own practical rationality. He has a rational engagement with the world in the sense that he reasons about what to do, makes judgments of what is choiceworthy, and acts accordingly. He has gotten things wrong, and if he is fixed in these policies of judgment and motivation, he may not be able to see his way clear of the errors. His exercise of reason is incorrect but not lesser.

Does this view of the relation between ethical disability and responsibility imply that there are things that the ethically disabled agent ought to do which he or she is unable to do? It does. The voluntarily ethically disabled agent is accountable for ethical failure, though there might have been no reasonable expectation that the agent could do what was ethically required. Yet, there are good reasons to doubt that the accessibility of an ethical requirement is a condition of an agent being responsible for action to which it is relevant.

In defending what he calls Aristotle's 'naturalism,' McDowell writes: "Those who serve in duty's army do not just happen to care about certain ends; we can say that reason reveals the dictates of virtue to them as genuine requirements on a rational will. The reason that effects this revelation is their acquired second nature. That this opens their eyes to real reasons for acting is argued not formally but materially, on the basis of Neurathian reflection that starts from the substantive view of the space of reasons opened up to them by their ethical upbringing. This makes it obviously wrong to expect right reason to be capable of issuing commands to just anyone, whatever his motivational make-up."[20] There are ethical requirements that are not recognized as such by ethically disabled agents and that is part of why they do not perceive their ethical failures as lapses. The Kantian rendering of 'ought implies can' presupposes that formal considerations of practical reason, considerations accessible to anyone who has not lost their reason, are sufficient to indicate ethical requirements. The 'can' is scaled up to what is categorically imperative by the presupposition of noumenal freedom. The rationality and accessibility of what is required is independent of any empirical features of character which are, in the present view, ineliminable conditions of practical reasoning that also affect the accessibility of ethical requirements.

Thomas Reid maintained a version of the doctrine that 'ought' implies 'can,' though with a qualification we do not find in Kant. Reid says, "it is a dictate of common sense, that we can be under no obligation to do what it is impossible for us to do."[21] He also observes that "In different men, the power of self-government is different, and in the same man at different times. It may be diminished, or perhaps lost, by bad habits; it may be greatly increased by good habits."[22] And, "Inveterate habits are acknowledged to diminish very considerably the power a man has over himself. Although we may think him highly blameable in acquiring them, yet when they are confirmed to a certain degree, we consider him as no longer master of himself, and hardly reclaimable without a miracle."[23] On the one hand, Reid defends a strong version of agent-causality and the capacity of agents to do what duty requires, which is also often intuitively evident, in his view. On the other hand, there is this suggestion that self-government can be undermined by bad habits and to such an extent that the agent is no longer a capable ethical agent. Reid seems to endorse the claim that 'ought implies can' and to also acknowledge that policies of self-government make a substantive difference to how successfully (in the moral sense) one exercises, and can exercise his agency. In his view, habits can disable an agent in such a way that it is no longer true that he ought to do something, because he cannot do it.

Habits can make a difference to whether one can do what one ought, without rendering the agent less responsible if the result is that "policies of self-government" degrade the agent's capacity for virtuous action. Maybe the agent cannot be reclaimed without a miracle, but he may still be fully an agent meriting accountability. His disability is, in a relevant sense, his own fault. In holding the agent accountable we can distinguish between his fault in becoming disabled and his fault in performing the wrong action. Given how he has disabled himself, it might be that he could not do otherwise in the case, though the character that makes necessary what he does is a character for which he bears an ethically significant measure of responsibility.

Both the wrong action and the character that underlies it are voluntary, though not in exactly the same way. Given the agent's character, there may be little else that is practically possible for him here and now. The point is not that at some earlier time various different ethically significant options were clear to him and because he chose badly, he is now confined to a defective ethical understanding. The different avenues presented to the agent may not have included ethically sound options or encouragement to pursue them. Rather, the point is that the agent has become the sort of agent he is through exercise of voluntariness. He is responsible for actions that express the values he endorses and the ends with which he identifies.

We might wish to say (as Reid seems to) that the agent is to blame for having become the sort of ethically defective agent he is, but that he is not to blame now for the failure to do what he ought, due to his inability. It may well be unreasonable to expect a vicious or disabled agent to do what he ought. But even when that expectation is inappropriate, the ethical requirement may still apply, and the agent is properly liable to blame. An individual who is fully an agent and who through exercise of his agency incapacitates himself for being moved by certain kinds of reasons is not thereby exempt from blame for not doing what those reasons require.

There are situations in which we say of an agent, "he ought to know (or have known) better," though it may be implausible that that very agent, with his history and character, *could* know or have known better. He ought to know better because he is not defective as an agent. That is, he is not defective except that we might say that he has ethical defects. He suffers from no constitutional incapacity to know better. This agent could have known better and acted better, if the 'could' is the generalized 'could' appropriate to human agents as a *kind* of being. As an agent in that sense it is appropriate to ascribe responsibility to him even though, as the particular agent he is, he may be alienated from ethical considerations in a way that limits what he can regard as action-guiding considerations. His not knowing better reflects limits that are grounded in his character and which, through his responsibility for character, are voluntary. He is a different kind of case from the individual who does know better but still acts wrongly, as a result of *akrasia*. That agent could have acted better in the sense that he did possess an understanding of what was ethically required, perhaps even recognized it as such, and failed to perform the right act though he was not prevented from doing so. He rightly sees this as a kind of inattention to the requirement or a failure on his part to follow through acting in the way that he believes he should, and it is a failure for which he is responsible.

It is part of Wolf's view that in order to be responsible for a wrong act, an agent must have been able to do the right thing for the right reasons. Blame and the full measure of responsibility are appropriate only where one fails to act well but had the ability to do so. She acknowledges that the excellent agent may not be able to act otherwise than virtuously. Her view of responsibility "does not entail that the agent have the unconditional ability to do otherwise. For it is possible that the agent who can do the right thing for the right reasons cannot do anything but that. In particular, an agent's vision may be so clear that she cannot help seeing which action is 'the right thing' and her virtue may be so sure that, knowing which action is right, she cannot help performing it."[24] Wolf holds that an agent is responsible for a good act which the agent could not help performing, while an agent is not responsible for a bad act which the agent could not help performing. I have presented reasons for reconsidering and adjusting this asymmetry.

The arguments of chapter 1 and this chapter call Wolf's view into question, at least if 'ability' means 'effective cognitive and motivational ability at the moment of action.' The agent's own history (of experience, choices, reactions, etc.), may so strongly fix a way of seeing things that at least some of the time, there is nothing else for the agent to do but what she does. Some things are out of the question even if they occur to the agent: others are not even thought of because they are not the kinds of considerations or possibilities that this sort of agent engages with.

Imagine, for example, a student who is particularly anxious about her academic record and who wants to take steps to ensure that she attains a certain grade level. Suppose someone points out that there is little time to dramatically improve her average and, really, the chances of moving up as much as she hopes to do are quite slim. This person might also point out that there is a quite reliable way to secure a counterfeit transcript, and perhaps that might be considered. Imagine that the student's reaction to this is to simply dismiss it (for it to go virtually unheard), not because it is too risky, but because it is dishonest. Her reaction is, "*What* are you saying? That is ridiculous; I can't do that." A student with a different character might consider it and reject it out of fear of discovery and penalty. Another might think it is a rather exciting idea and one that promises a swift resolution to her worries about her record, with all of the dramatic appeal of breaking the rules. The possibility appears to her as a revelation of what she of course should do. The virtuous student who is 'deaf' to the suggestion may not be able to act otherwise, because of her character. That, Wolf agrees, is plainly not a reason for diminished responsibility. My claim is that neither would a background of cheating, deception, corner-cutting and dishonesty be an excusing consideration, even if the student had been 'trained' in these things by upbringing. Maybe this individual thinks that such practices are the ways to get ahead in a competitive, each-for-oneself environment and that cheating is part of "how the game is played, if you are not a sucker." The disposition to see things in this way and to be motivated in this way may be so firm as to effectively occlude any other view. In that case, there is an ability to act for the right reasons in only the thinnest of senses; it is not an ability that that agent could effectively engage in that situation.

Consider another example. Suppose a young man loses his parents and is sent to live with relatives. And suppose that this new environment is not a particularly salutary one. The uncle sometimes treats the aunt abusively, and the cousins are frequently in trouble at school and in minor scrapes with the law. The uncle and aunt feel some responsibility for looking after this new member of their household but also feel some resentment. It is a financial burden that they are not well prepared to handle, and their affection for their orphaned nephew is grudging and takes erratic forms that confuse him. He is a capable student but irregular in his efforts and attendance, and he does far less well than his teachers believe that he is able to do. After a while he begins to exhibit the pattern of mischief-making characteristic of his cousins. He becomes an occasional binge drinker and is dismissed from a series of jobs for theft of goods, absence from work, and other kinds of irresponsible behavior. Imagine him going on in this way, with the pattern becoming more evident and his difficulties at employment, with the law, and in personal relationships increasing. Is this someone who on account of his misfortune is less responsible for his actions and character than he would be if he did not suffer such misfortune?

With so many reasons for unhappiness and such a lack of guidance, the resources and occasions for corruption of character are in ample supply. The inducements to act in ways that establish bad habits surely help explain the unhappy history of this man. Granted, there was not a point at which he set out to have less-than-virtuous tendencies and dispositions; still, they are results of his voluntary activity. The vices he has acquired were not imposed upon him, though we can understand his susceptibility to them. Plainly, the influences that dominated the formation of his second nature were wanting in respect to ethical soundness. Nonetheless, these factors do not cause him to be a less responsible agent. In order for him to be responsible for what he does and for what he is like, he need not have had the actual, practical option of being habituated or influenced more positively. That might have (it almost surely would have) made a difference to what sort of person he became, but not in terms of his being someone more responsible for his actions.

Wolf argues that "Whatever the explanation that prevents the agent from being able to do the right thing for the right reasons, our intuitions seem to support the claim that the agent does not deserve blame. If an agent is incapable of doing the right thing for the right reasons, then it is not her fault that she stumbles into doing something wrong."[25] It is not clear that the "whatever the explanation" clause belongs there. An agent whose capacities are defective is a quite different case from an agent whose capacities are established in bad patterns. Granted, if you have had bad luck with respect to habituation and the transmission of values, and you do not understand why your actions and dispositions are ethically disordered, then there may be nowhere for you to go (in the sense of effectively *being able to go there*). Due to your lack of understanding you are confined to a narrowness of vision in which you cannot see what is right or good. You are not though, lesser as an agent.

In many cases it may be plausible that the person who comes to be ethically disabled *ought*, as a rational agent, *to have seen* that certain practices and motivational policies are ethically unsound. The agent may have failed to pay attention to the consequences of his actions for his own character or may have made no effort to envision different values. This is not to say that everyone can be expected to foresee what his or her regular practices will lead to in the establishment of character and that everyone should be able to effectively critically examine prevailing values. I have argued that such a position would be unreasonable. Still, the fact that an individual is habituated in a certain way or the fact that there are certain prevailing attitudes does not release the agent from responsibility for acquiring the characteristics and value commitments that constitute his mature character.

If Hitler's parents had loved him in better ways, or if Germany had been victorious in the First World War and he thought all was right with the world, or if he had had friends who succeeded in distracting him from his fanatical hatreds and ideological fantasies, then, tautologically, he would have had a different story, and he might well have had different concerns and projects. Even if we grant that he would have acted differently had his story been different, the fact that his story helps explain his wild, murderous views does not imply that his actual story is a responsibility-defeating cause of what he actually did and the sort of person he became.

DISABILITY, SANITY, AND RESPONSIBILITY

Wolf says that "the slaveowner, the Nazi, or the male chauvinist . . . are unable cognitively and normatively to recognize and appreciate the world for what it is. In our sense of the term, their deepest selves are not fully *sane*."[26] Because they are not fully sane, in her view, they are also not responsible for their actions: "Since these characters lack the ability to know right from wrong, they are unable to revise their characters on the basis of right and wrong, and so their deep selves lack the resources and the reasons that might have served as a basis for self-correction."[27] That may be, though it is not a reason for doubting their sanity. To do so would improperly discount the role of compliance, desire, and endorsement in the development of their characters. Their understanding of how to find their way around the moral landscape is disfigured, but the paths that they follow are paths that they follow voluntarily and through the exercise of reason. Again, the main point is not that their ethical defects are entirely their own fault but that these individuals have been and remain responsible as practical reasoners and voluntary agents. We can judge that an agent is responsible even if it seems pretty clear to us that he or she of course acts that way, given the agent's 'story' (as in the case of the slaveowner). The 'of course' is not an abbreviation for saying that there was less responsibility involved in the act but for the intelligibility of *this* person acting *that* way. The inability to act in accordance with the True and the Good (Wolf's formulation) may be an indication of how important habituation is rather than a basis for diminishing responsibility for character and action. It is correct to stress the importance of cognition and control for virtue and for good action. Yet, there is no incoherence in the conjunction of the thoughts "the agent is responsible" and "what did you expect?" whether we are referring to virtue that we praise or to vice that we deplore.

The child who was raised on Nazi indoctrination and propaganda and who took up the cause with enthusiasm was in certain respects prevented from seeing things in any other way. At home, in school, in clubs and organizations, the ideology was impressed upon him, and the measures and symbols of honor, success, status, and the like were shaped to conform to Nazi ideology. This is a dubious form of moral education, to say the least, but it is distinguishable from say, the brainwashing of a prisoner of war or the destruction of a juvenile's capacity for ethical personality and responsible action by deprivation of experience, learning, and social interaction. The abilities that are the abilities of responsible agents were present in the individual raised in Nazi Germany (and Nazi Austria, and the other places where Nazism was embraced. We should not think of the Nazi phenomenon as a localized phenomenon). This is still an agent who could use a repertoire of ethically relevant concepts (of justice, generosity, fidelity, courage, resolve) even if there is a substantial measure of perversity in his understanding of how they apply. My main point is not that Nazis and their followers, for example, should have been expected to see the immorality of it all. As a matter of fact, many of them did but participated anyway or did not do anything about it. They condoned, allowed, or at least failed to protest what was going on. Though there were very powerful forces at work encouraging acceptance of and enthusiasm for Nazi ideology and though there were substantial risks in opposing it, those who took up the Nazi cause or acquiesced in it were often no less morally responsible for their actions or failures to act. Some were weak, some were vicious, and some were ethically disabled. There were many victims and many kinds of victims of the Nazis. Other Nazis and Nazi supporters fit in the category of 'victim' in a different sense, if at all.

DISABILITY AND BLAME

The view we are criticizing seems to move from an intuition about when it is appropriate to lessen *blame* to a conclusion that certain agents are therefore less responsible. My suggestion is that our notion of what it is to fully be an agent supports a different reading of the situation. Even lessening blame may not be appropriate. If we lessen blame, presumably that is because the agency of this person is somehow diminished.

Consider again Wolf's example of the slaveowner. The Georgia slaveowner of 1850 is a no less responsible agent than the citizens of Georgia today, though we may blame him differently for his racist attitudes than we would blame today's racist. This is not because having those views in 1850 was any less bad or wrong. The truth-value of "Slavery (of the type present in Georgia in 1850) is morally wrong" does not depend upon what time it is, though it is in certain ways more obnoxious and ugly to have such views now. An agent today should be more reachable with regard to its immorality and the spuriousness of the beliefs that under-wrote support for slavery. However, it is not clear that agents who harbor such views now are also somehow more responsible, more voluntary in doing so, than their counterparts at an earlier time.

By 'blame' we might just mean the fact that the person was the agent of wrongdoing; that he, and not someone else, is 'to blame.' And indeed, the slaveowners of 1850 are to blame for the evils of the slave system at that time. But we also mean by 'blame' a mode of address to the wrong-doer by which the agent might be motivated to acknowledge his wrong and make an effort of self-correction. Blame is not just a matter of point-ing to 'who did it' but also an approach to the agent that involves a certain kind of morally significant relation to him. Blaming is also a way of being true to our values. Even though Reinhard Heydrich, Pol Pot, or members of the Ku Klux Klan may be impervious to blame and criticism, there is still an ethical point in blaming them. We blame Heydrich, Pol Pot, and the Imperial Wizard because of their viciousness, even though it is most unlikely that they would make an effort to correct themselves or acknowl-edge the correctness of the values that sanction blaming them. These are agents who are blameworthy though they cannot be expected to respond in ethically sound ways to being blamed.

As a mode of ethically addressing someone, blame typically presup-poses that the agent is susceptible to acknowledging the reasons that make his act wrong and is thereby susceptible to changing his action-guid-ing conceptions and dispositions. The person who feels guilty and responds in an ethically healthy manner has been moved by that suscepti-bility. Of course, even many ethically capable agents will not *in fact* be so moved, though that does not nullify the ethical point of blame. An ethi-cally disabled agent is not susceptible to realizing his guilt or acknowledg-ing his wrong because of the fixity of his dispositions (both judgmentally and motivationally). It is not that he is thereby excused in some manner, but that *we* would be unreasonable in expecting (or demanding, whatever that might mean) that he see things in the right way. His ethical disability cuts us off from effectively reaching him in certain ways.

There are barriers apart from the obvious temporal one (for example, distancing us from slave owners in 1850) to effective communication of moral reasons between groups with significantly different entrenched habits of judgment and valuation. The non-temporal barriers are much too simply characterized if they are attributed to the irrationality of one of the groups. It is true that we may wonder what is the point of blame, insofar as those agents cannot be expected to respond to blame with an acknowledgment of error and an effort at self-correction. This *does* make it difficult to judge whether blame is appropriate and can confuse us regarding just what we are undertaking in blaming. However, this difficulty is not resolved by simply lessening blame and, correlatively, diminishing responsibility. The disruption to our reactive attitudes and judgments that is caused by other agents' ethical disability cannot be eliminated in that way. We have to live with the perplexity and the disruption it causes. The uneasiness is not evidence of incoherence in our judgments of responsibility. It is evidence of the way in which ethical disability challenges our ethical understanding. In regard to agents of another time, our focus may shift from blame to the attempt to understand why those agents held the values that they held. There is not the same sort of urgent practical relation that there is with people with whom we have to live together in the world. It is not that we are simply exculpating the former or diluting their responsibility. In both remote and proximate instances we often cannot confidently settle on a mode of ethical approach to them until we better understand their valuative attachments, which are unsound, and for that very reason, especially difficult to understand. And we may never reach a point where we feel that the perverse values are explained in such a way that the agents' responsibility is lessened, or in such a way that we can fully appreciate their endorsement of those values.

We may feel that others with quite different values are not in a common moral world shared with us. That is a kind of denial. They *are* a part of our moral world, though in a perhaps unwelcome and very disturbing way. In some respects they are far away. Their world was (or is) quite different from our own. Still, we should not conclude that people are less than fully responsible for acting on values that are deeply perverse or wrong. That *would be* a form of denial. Indeed, part of the interest that we have in societal conditions such as the institution of slavery, or fascist politics and the culture that produces and encourages such a state, is that it is our world in which these conditions are found.

Consider someone raised by parents who are bigots and who lives in a largely homogeneous community in which certain sorts of bigotry are well entrenched. These values are passed on through the generations; in fact, opposition to them is regarded with suspicion and hostility by the majority. Let's suppose that this agent participates in an act of vandalism motivated by his bigotry. On the other hand, consider another individual, from a background free of those vices, who commits what, on the face of it, is a very similar crime. He is not motivated by resentment, cruelty, or malice. He participates in an act of vandalism because he is "pushed into it" by friends who think of it as exciting and as a test of nerve and guts. Both agents are adults. While in one sense, their acts are equally blameworthy, in another sense we may legitimately wonder if blaming them similarly and *responding* to them in the same manner makes the most moral sense. Each is a responsible agent but our moral relations to them differ. This is because the first agent is so fixed in error or vice that he will not endorse the values that rationalize blaming him.

The ethically disabled agent may refuse to involve himself in the process of blame by refusing to acknowledge his wrong, any need to make it right, any need to ask forgiveness, and any need for an effort of self-correction. He may not credit the reasons for being blamed, in which case of course he does not see it supplying him a reason to reassess himself and his conduct, except perhaps prudentially. The second agent does credit them. His error is a lapse of moral judgment or composure. His act is traceable to a kind of weakness. The fact that the first agent is unresponsive to the relevant ethical considerations should not deflect blame; it is still merited. But if we are thinking of it as more than just a report to the wrongdoer that we denounce his act or find his character obnoxious, then we may be unclear about how blame is to be addressed to this agent.

A well-supported, informed expectation that blame will not reach the agent in a morally efficacious manner (I don't mean this in a consequentialist sense but in terms of the understanding of blame by the person blamed) can leave us perplexed. The perplexity is not so much about the legitimacy of blame but about the gap between the reasons that support issuing it and the lack of receptivity to it, on account of indifference to, or rejection of, those reasons.[28] Blame can be a way of including the wrongdoer in the common moral world, not just a mode of condemnation or denunciation. It can reflect fidelity to true values for that world. There are unclarities concerning how we show respect to the agent being punished, and fidelity to our values, while recognizing that the agent will not and maybe cannot endorse those values. This, though, is a difficulty about how to address the agent, about just what approach to the agent is ethically appropriate given that he is responsible and blameworthy. It is not primarily a difficulty about whether the agent is responsible or blameworthy.

In *The Nature of Morality*, Harman's discussion of moral reasons implies one kind of approach to this perplexity. He writes: "In saying that it was wrong of Hitler to have ordered the extermination of the Jews we would be saying that Hitler had a reason (every reason in the world) not to do what he did. But what is horrible about someone who did what he did is that he could not have had such a reason. If he was willing to exterminate a whole people, there was no reason for him not to do so: that is just what is so terrible about him."[29] A bit later he says, "Hitler, like the cannibals, is outside our morality, although in a different direction. We can judge his acts with reference to our morality, but not Hitler himself, since that would imply that he was someone who acknowledged the moral standards we use to judge him."[30]

This view gives the agent the option of locating himself beyond the reach of blame (in a sense of blame other than just, "he is the one who did it") by not acknowledging the values that rationalize it. The agent absents himself from the proceedings by not sharing the principles of those who blame him. Harman may be correct in noting that a practice such as blame or claiming that it is wrong for an agent to do such and such will have no moral traction with agents whose principles are very different from those who issue the judgments. Because of the agent's ethical disability *we* are unable to rationally influence him. We should not conclude from the failure of blame to reach the agent that the agent is not wrong to act in the way he does or that he is not blameworthy. These facts are not, however, evidence for the truth of relativism. We cannot pursue that issue in depth here, though our moral psychological claims will be supported by arguments for a realist metaethics in chapter 5.

The present account takes very seriously the fact that different agents accept different kinds of considerations as good reasons and it acknowledges that in not being attuned to correct ethical considerations on account of his character, an agent may reject what in fact are true ethical considerations as having no claim on him as a rational agent. Thus, he is not susceptible to certain kinds of regret or shame nor motives for self-correction on the right terms. In this state, the agent is rational, but unreachable by the rational appeals that do reach other agents, due to reasons he considers sound.

DISABILITY AND RETRIBUTION

The argument so far has presented a conception of responsibility that has a quite 'natural' fit with certain retributivist views. It has not been the aim of the account to make a case for retributivism, and this is not the place for a full-scale exploration of it, particularly as an issue of legal sanction for violations of criminal law. The main concern here is responsibility, not punishment. None the less, the position can be helpfully elaborated by considering the debate about retributivist considerations, and in partricular, their relation to what we have said about blame and the larger moral psychology in which those claims are embedded.

Retributive sentiments can be as appropriate, as rationally legitimate as sentiments of gratitude or admiration, and, like those, they can be well placed or not.[31] We should not think of retributivism as primarily an orderly way to express rage or disgust or vengefulness. There is a rationale for retributivist considerations that is not limited to 'dealing with' negative and unconstructive reactions to wrongdoing which need a safe outlet. Granted, retributive sentiments can be very undisciplined and dangerous. But there is an ethically legitimate place for resentment of wrongdoing. Moreover, our moral sentiments are not so plastic that they can be redirected to quite different ends.

It might be argued that we should convert the energy of outrage, for example, into something more positive and engage it to policies and practices aimed at promoting social welfare—and perhaps even that this conversion should result in the replacement of retributive sentiments and not just the redeployment of them. I think such an attempt is bound to fail, not because people will always be vengeful, but because it depends upon an incorrect reading of the ethical legitimacy of certain kinds of retributive sentiments. Compare the case to the cases of admiration and gratitude. Failure to admire or to be grateful can be symptomatic of an ethical flaw that is not merely a matter of feeling. It is reflective of what sorts of valuations the agent makes and what sorts of considerations rationalize reactions and attitudes to others. Similarly, retributive sentiments can be guided by correct or incorrect judgments of what is merited by the actions of agents. It is a misunderstanding to interpret them as passions that always lead and never follow judgment and as passions that it would be best to be rid of because there is so little in them to admire.[32] Retribution *can* seem to be 'good for nothing' and an unconstructive response to wrongdoing. If it is thought of as no more than returning evil for evil then it does look morally unpromising. However, it should be thought of not just in terms of applying punitive sanction, but in terms of the moral grounds that legitimate doing so.

Jean Hampton, in *Forgiveness and Mercy,* says that "retribution isn't about making a criminal better; it is about denying a false claim of relative value."[33] And "genuinely nonmalicious retributivists have as the aim behind the infliction of suffering not the vengeful diminishment of the criminal to a bestial level but the vindication of the victim's value."[34] She acknowledges that the retributivist "wants the moral truth to be heard, but is not intent on successful persuasion or criminal reform; he wants to annul the criminal's message and reassert the moral truth, but does not perceive punishment as a certain cure for immorality."[35] This is a way of sustaining the point and legitimacy of retribution, while recognizing that it may not yield gains in any of the senses that typically come under the heading of 'social benefit.' The retributivist can of course want and welcome whatever good (in a more consequentialist sense) comes of punishment.

Still, a question can be raised about what has been annulled if the character of the person punished silences the justification of the punishment. If punishment does not (except symbolically) annul the crime or reconnect the offender to true values or if it carries out only an expressive function,[36] is there still a sufficient rationale to underwrite retributivist considerations? What if neither the offender nor the victim believes that the moral truth has been reasserted? I think we should try to understand retributivist considerations in a way that does not depend upon responses of these kinds to such an extent that the practice of punishment risks becoming *merely* symbolic. Although it is crucial that the values that retributive sanction enacts are sound values, it is not essential that everyone liable to sanction actually acknowledge the soundness of those values. Punitive sanctioning of even those who are ethically disabled (as a result of voluntary activity) would be permissible, though there is slim expectation or even grounds for hope that they will come to endorse the values that legitimate sanctioning them.

Often, even where there is doubt that punishment will have good effects, we have the reasoned conviction that punishment is warranted and just, and this is not just because we want to even the scales or pay back the wrongdoer. It is not a matter of being wedded to such metaphors.[37] In part, it is because of the voluntary agency expressed by the action of the wrongdoer acting as a responsible agent. The agent brought some evil into the world, did so willingly, and it is the fitness of our resentment of that, and not the likelihood of changing the wrongdoer that ethically rationalizes punishment.[38] The reassertion of moral truth may indeed often be mainly symbolic. There are, though, other grounds for retributivism that are not susceptible to being so. Retributively rationalized punishment can assert true values, but the rightness of the assertion is not dependent upon the spirit in which the assertion is heard.

The ethically disabled agent may be the sort of person who thinks "you can blame and punish me, but it will not make any difference," and he is not just making a prediction, but a correct point about the steadiness of his convictions or the firmness of his character. Even if he does not explicitly have that thought, he may be the sort of agent who will not respond to punishment by acknowledging its justice (supposing it to be just) and undertaking to reform himself. He may recognize that what he has done is regarded as the ground for his liability to punishment (either as a violation of criminal law or a violation of the moral standards accepted by those with authority to punish) but still not acknowledge the warrant for punishment. He can see what is coming but does not credit it as deserved, and he remains untroubled by guilt. Nonetheless, however disordered his moral conceptions may be, it may be appropriate that the agent be punished (rather than exempted from it or required to undergo therapeutic treatment). In reflecting upon retributive sentiments and their ethical place, we should think not only of what punishment typically brings about but also of what motivates those sentiments and the extent to which it is appropriate for them to supply reasons for action. Blaming and punishing may fail to do good in terms of consequences but may still be ethically apt on account of the valuative considerations they enact. Thus, they may be appropriately addressed to responsible but ethically disabled agents.

Part of what is so disturbing and perplexing about deeply and persistently vicious people is that they can act with so much naturalness and lack of motivational conflict. How could they do *that*, or be like *that*, and not feel conflict or remorse? When we wonder at these things we are doing more than expressing anger or vengefulness. We are also expressing confusion and frustration that moral demands are met with indifference or contempt by responsible agents with whom we have to live in the world.[39] Agents may be unrepentant or reject the significance of ethical considerations, because they are so fully alienated from a sound appreciation of good that they are effectively inaccessible. Appeals to conscience or to a sense of decency or justice may be unavailing in attempts to change those being punished. We feel both the appropriateness of retributive sentiments and the worry that policies based upon them may be "good for nothing" with respect to improving the agents who are sanctioned. There is here, a blurriness on the ethical landscape because of the lack of congruence between the agent's responsibility and his ability to know better or to change. This is a blurriness we have to live with. It would be a mistake to eliminate it by contracting the responsibility of agents.

Granted, to hold others responsible is not *necessarily* a stance that gives a central place to retributive sentiments, or at least they need not ethically trump all other ethical considerations.[40] Still, the view presented here can help explain why, in spite of the difficulties they bring with them, there is a proper place for retributive considerations in morality and in the justification of punishment. The retributivist may hope for recognition of wrongdoing and reform on the part of the person punished, but that these should occur (or occur in all but quite exceptional cases) is not necessary as part of the rationale for retributivism. If character typically becomes fixed, there may be much less prospect of punishment effectively motivating penance and reform than we would like to think. And the fact that punishment will not improve a person or that it will not be recognized as ethically warranted by that person are not considerations that (in any obvious or conceptually mandated way) ethically disqualify punishment.

In the next chapter we will continue to explore the relation between character and ethical cognition. We will take up more directly the issue of whether an agent can change his character to an ethically significant extent. The discussion will reinforce the view we have been developing that indeed agents can become and remain ethically disabled.

CHAPTER 3

Ethical Accessibility and Plasticity of Character

In this chapter we will explore in more depth the issue of whether agents are able to revise their habits of thought and motivation in the direction of virtue. This is ethical self-correction, or, in the older idiom, repentance and reform, but without supernatural grace. If this is possible, as a matter of the ability of agents in general, then even those with long-established vicious characters should be able to reorient themselves toward virtue. The arguments of the first two chapters point to the conclusion that such a view is overly optimistic. The combined effect of the role of character in ethical cognition and the tendency of character to become fixed is threefold. First, it is not true that the realized capacity to correctly grasp ethical considerations is a condition of responsible agency. Second, there are agents we should not expect to overcome ethical disability. Finally, it is not true in a completely general way that 'ought' implies 'can.'

Much of the case for these conclusions has already been presented. Still, we might think that even if there are limits on the plasticity of a mature agent's character, the capacities that come with rational maturity might enable the agent to change in the direction of virtue. One's developed practical rationality plus the learning one has acquired in experience might seem to position the agent to do this. So, even if we stand by the first of the claims above, perhaps the second and third should be revised or rejected. Yet, I will argue that we should be quite modest in our expectations with respect to character change. The modest prospects for character change supply additional support for the claim that some agents are ethically disabled in ways they cannot overcome.

To more fully explicate the relation between plasticity of character and ethical ability we will examine some of the differences between the present view and the moral psychology and moral epistemology found in the works of Maimonides.[1] This may sound an odd choice. Maimonides is a medieval; his works are not widely known, and interest in them is usually weighted to his theological claims and arguments rather than to his moral psychology. I have selected him because the contrast between Maimonides and Aristotle is particularly relevant to the present set of issues. Again, the view we are presenting is not being attributed to Aristotle, but it does borrow extensively from him, so the contrast between it and the Maimonidean view will be instructive. Maimonides and Aristotle share a great deal concerning moral psychology, but Maimonides believes that agents with long-established vices can ethically self-correct. He takes this stand without appealing to any non-natural agency or to grace in order to change character. Among philosophers heavily influenced by Aristotle, Aquinas is much better known, but there is a role for grace in his account of virtue that marks a significant departure from Aristotle's view.[2] Exploring the contrast between Aristotle and Maimonides is a particularly effective way to highlight the nature of ethical disability and to focus on whether 'ought' implies 'can.' In addition, notwithstanding Maimonides' explicit theological commitments, his view has important affinities to more modern and secular views about the accessibility of ethical requirements and the relation of that issue to moral psychology. So, this is not mainly an exercise in comparative historical study, but a way to make more explicit and vivid a debate that has a long history and that straddles religious and secular approaches.

HOW MUCH CHANGE MAKES FOR CHANGE OF CHARACTER?

Before turning to the contrast between Aristotle and Maimonides and its implications, some preliminary remarks are needed concerning just what sorts of change in an agent's character are of chief concern for present purposes. It must be allowed that this is difficult terrain to map in a definitive way. There are changes in dispositions that do not really constitute a change of character in the relevant sense either because the changes are not enduring or because they are not changes in ethically significant features of the agent. The sort of change that matters here is a change in an agent's effectively action-guiding conceptions of value and his dispositions to act on them. A change in manner or the way one presents oneself, even if it is quite striking does not count as a change in character.

Enduring and motivating valuative conceptions and our fidelity to them supply the basis of many of our judgments of self-worth, our valuations of the acts and characters of others, feelings of remorse, assessments of the worthwhileness of our undertakings, and the like. For example, the gossip referred to in chapter 1 who gave up the practice may have done so as part of a reflective, deliberate project of trying to revise his character. Perhaps he began to see gossip as emblematic of a certain kind of shallowness he wanted to repudiate. There are other reasons why someone might give up being a gossip that have little to do with the agent's reflection on his character and ethical concern. Perhaps his interest and attention are now directed elsewhere; maybe flattery is more profitable. So it is not just the pattern of behavior that is at issue but also what it counts for to the agent in terms of fundamental practical value.

Sometimes a change in circumstances or opportunities brings out efforts, attitudes, and concerns that the agent did not formerly exhibit. Dealing with unaccustomed adversity may have this result, and so may unaccustomed good fortune.[3] For example, we may find out that an individual, freed of the stress of material insecurity, is really quite generous and solicitous of others, having previously been much more self-centered. Is that a change of character, or really just a change in which features of character are expressed in the most pronounced manner? Is it only a change in mood or feeling but not quite a change in character? Or imagine a person who has long exhibited a kind of self-important insouciance and easy-going manner who then undergoes a reversal of fortune and becomes more humble and shows more concern for others. This may not actually be a genuine or deep change in his character. It could be, for example, evidence of a basic, consistent feature of character; namely, his outlook and attitude toward other people and their predicaments are very substantially influenced by his own fortune. He is someone who is particularly sensitive to circumstantial luck.

Consider another type of case. Suppose an agent has a history of alcohol and drug abuse and criminal behavior, but, while in prison, he becomes a model prisoner, pursues educational opportunities, and works hard at trying to get other prisoners to 'turn themselves around' and live clean, decent lives. Is this a significant change in character, or is it an expression of character out from under the influence of drugs and alcohol and the unhappy facts of life that drove this person to drugs and alcohol? How much is a change in environment an enabling condition for bringing out aspects of character, and how much is an environmental change a cause of more substantial changes in character? When a person changes for the better in significant ways it can be very difficult to ascertain whether the positive change occurs because conditions are now favorable to bringing out the good that was in him or because he is making dramatically new acknowledgments and recomposing his character.

We can make some important general claims about moral psychology without achieving conclusive answers to these questions. In any case, in speaking of changing character, we need not mean the agent's entire character but a change in mature dispositions that is an ethically significant change reflected in more than just one narrow type of judgment, practice, or reaction. It would be a change that is not isolated or compartmentalized or superficial. For example, the continent agent may be able to change by efforts to become more firmly virtuous. That should count as a change in character, if indeed the agent really has 'silenced' motives that earlier had real energy. On the other hand, someone may become much more well mannered or polite, for example, though this is not because he has really become a more considerate and decent person. He may still be devious or malicious. Indeed, that may be what is behind the change in manner; he can more successfully deceive and swindle others by being more genial.

Even supposing we could be quite definite about what constitutes a change in character, we have to ask: Do one's own voluntarily established dispositions dramatically limit the capacity for change of the relevant kind through limiting practical vision and through the conservatism of habit? Can a person acquire a second nature more than once when doing so would require plasticity of character (imaginative, motivational, judgmental, affective) such that it can be responsive to ethical considerations in a significantly different way? Even with rational capacities, plainly, we cannot ethically 'drydock' our characters and suspend our cognitive and motivational dispositions. Not even reason is a capacity enabling us to do that. This is especially so if serious vices are long established.

Although I do not wish to rule out ethically significant character change I will argue that rational agency does not ensure capacity for ethical self-correction. The fact that we are rational agents is not sufficient to underwrite the possibility of character change in a completely general way. Yes, the continent agent may become more firmly virtuous. And yes, an agent with vices can make what we have reason to believe are genuine changes in the direction of virtue. There are still reasons to conclude that there are responsible ethically disabled agents who are disabled in the sense that virtue is not a practical possibility for them. The difficulty of the change is enlarged by the inability to bring into view what it would require. Also, we should observe that whatever the possibility or difficulty of changing one's character, there are many, many people to whom this course does not occur. They do not raise for themselves the issue of whether character change is something they should try to undertake.

The objection could be made that this view holds people responsible for their luck in an especially unfair and ungenerous way. Perhaps there are differences in capacity for character change just as there are differences in temperament, which makes the acquisition of virtue more or less difficult. In addition, the influences to which one has been subject can powerfully impact aspiration, the sense of what is possible, and the scope and character of one's self-reflections. So, on the one hand, it seems that some agents do undergo changes in character, and, on the other hand, perhaps many of those who do not change for the better are not able to, and their inability should lessen their responsibility for the characters they have. Here are quite different kinds of reasons converging on the conclusion that we should reconsider our claims about ethical disability. Perhaps in general people are capable of bringing about changes in their characters, but when they are not, this is largely due to luck. Are there good grounds to maintain the claim that there are responsible, ethically disabled agents who are disabled for ethically recomposing themselves? Are there agents whose inability to change is not mainly a matter of bad luck? The reasons for thinking that there are indeed agents in that category are what we need to explore.

THE ARISTOTELIAN BACKGROUND TO THE VIEW

In discussing character change, as in the discussion of voluntariness, Aristotle is a good starting point. His view is that there are ethically important features of an agent's character that are not innate. They are acquired, but, once acquired and established, they are resistant to change. In the process of maturation there is plasticity during the establishment of characteristics, but that plasticity is very much diminished with the passage of time. Of course, second nature can be revealed and expressed in unexpected ways, and the fixity of character does not imply that we can always confidently predict how someone will act (even in our own cases). The 'quiet man' who just goes about his business may surprise us with his capacity for violence or cruelty. Or the disreputable character may surprise us with unselfishness and generosity. In such cases, it is not as if the agent's character has undergone some episode of major change. We just did not know the person as well as we thought or we did not anticipate the way in which he would respond to circumstances. Additionally, even though character typically becomes fixed, this does not imply that the agent's character does not have complex texture. Fixity does not always bring with it harmony or absence of conflict. Indeed, most of us are neither firmly nor uniformly fixed in virtue or vice. We are in the crowded 'mixed' space between them.

For example, we may go on feeling unwanted passions and desires but manage them in ways that can be called continent. The ongoing struggle with them (and periodically succumbing to them) may itself become a fixed feature of character. Someone may need years of adult life and experience to figure out how to manage resentment or how to be less self-centered, or how to recognize the ways in which he has been less than fully honest or courageous, but he may still fail to fully overcome the inclination to dishonesty or cowardice. Or imagine an agent with a temperament that favors certain virtues, but it does not seem important to him that he should have those virtues in a full-fledged way. He may be capable of real concern for others and may sometimes exhibit determination in helping them but not with the firmness of disposition and steadiness of commitment that are marks of virtue. His virtue seems to be haphazard. He seems like someone who could really have the virtues, but his sensitivity is erratic, and he lacks concern to fully make the virtues his own, being satisfied with his own way. He is not bothered by this, whereas other agents are troubled by their inconsistency of disposition. Fixity of character does not imply that the agent has the various virtues or vices in roughly equal degree, or that the agent is relatively free of conflict and can live with himself without finding it painful. Still, once character is established, it is through those habits of judgment, motivation, and sentiment that the agent addresses and reacts to the world. And even if there is a desire to change, the already formed material of character may resist the effort.

For Aristotle fixity was important to both virtue and vice in that the full-fledged presence of each involves the relevant states being established as second nature. Fixity of character is important also to his conceptions of happiness, friendship, and self-love. The stability of happiness depends upon the stability of virtue, that is, the stability of character. (See, for example, *NE* 1100b7–35, and bk. 10, chap. 6.) Without fixity of character, the stability of happiness would be much more vulnerable to the shocks of misfortune. In the best friendships, excellent agents desire and act for the sake of the good of other excellent agents, and all appreciate the enduring goodness of their virtuous characters. They appreciate goodness both in the sense of valuing and taking pleasure in it and also in the reciprocal sense of receiving good from it on account of the friend's excellent activity. It is true that the character of a person of even outstanding virtue can change if tragedy and suffering make it almost humanly impossible to maintain moral composure. But, for stably virtuous agents, what may be most changed is whether their lives are happy rather than whether their characters are virtuous. (See *NE* 1100b20–1101a14.) There is a kind of durability to mature, deeply grounded virtue such that the quality of the life of an excellent agent may be degraded without the agent's character being corrupted. There is also durability to ethical disability owing to the agent's lack or loss of practical vision. Also, as we indicated in chapter 2, the ethically disabled agent may not even be susceptible to the self-hatred and internal conflict that Aristotle took to be a penalty for vice.

Even apart from Aristotle's teleological commitments and their normative concomitants it is fairly plain that agents' characters do typically become quite firmly fixed. There is an ensemble of values, commitments, attitudes, and sensibility that a mature agent settles into, and that ensemble is generally not much altered or disturbed, even though it may be difficult to describe, and it may undergo certain sorts of 'natural' changes at different times of life, with different features being more or less pronounced. Mature reflection may bring realizations that cause regret and motivate efforts at change. But even the combination of rationality and experience may not guarantee the capacity to reconstitute second nature. One's habits of valuation and reasoning can put some kinds of options, aspirations, understandings out of reach. That is not indicative of diminished rationality or the constraints of fortune.

An important upshot of the account of ethical disability is that if 'ought' implies 'can' in a completely general way, then either agents must be capable of a significant departure from established character in order to do what is morally required (and, of course, must first be able to recognize that it *is* morally required), or diminished responsibility is to be ascribed to many agents whose characters are fixed, because they are not capable of seeing and doing what virtue requires. But there is an inadequate rationale for saving 'ought implies can' in either of those ways. Kant, for example, held that "when the moral law commands that we *ought* now to be better men, it follows inevitably that we must *be able* to be better men."[4] And, "From the practical point of view this idea [the moral ideal] is completely real in its own right, for it resides in our morally-legislative reason. We *ought* to conform to it; consequently we must *be able* to do so."[5] There are reasons to think that this is an implausible idealization of moral agency. Some of those reasons we have already examined, others will be presented below.

A VARIANT OF THE ARISTOTELIAN VIEW

Maimonides' views are directly relevant to the debate about whether 'ought' implies 'can.' His moral psychology is like Aristotle's in many respects, but he is also more optimistic about the capacity of agents to revise their characters in the direction of virtue. While Maimonides believes that moral law has a divine source, he also believes that human beings are responsible for their characters and that the extent to which they possess moral virtue depends upon their own efforts. Even though his ethics involves a theistic metaphysics, he has an understanding of redemptive possibility, of the possibility of change of character in the direction of virtue, which it is not inappropriate to call 'naturalistic.'

Like Aristotle, Maimonides denies that we have the virtues and vices by nature. "It is not possible for a man to possess virtue or vice by nature, from the beginning of his life, just as it is not possible for man to possess one of the practical arts by nature. Still, it is possible to be naturally disposed toward a virtue or a vice, so that it is easier to perform the actions that accord with a [particular virtue] or a [particular vice]."[6] As Aristotle does, Maimonides puts a great deal of weight on habituation as a formative factor with respect to character: "Know that these moral virtues and vices are acquired and firmly established in the soul by frequently repeating the actions pertaining to a particular moral habit over a long period of time and by our becoming accustomed to them."[7] And again, as Aristotle does, Maimonides characterizes the virtues as lying in a mean between excess and defect: "Good actions are those balanced in the mean between two extremes, both of which are bad; one of them is an excess and the other a deficiency. The virtues are states of the soul and settled dispositions in the mean between two bad states [of the soul], one of which is excessive and the other deficient."[8] Finally, he too, has a perfectionist conception of human nature, centered on the perfection of man as a rational being.[9]

While Maimonides acknowledges that one might be naturally disposed toward a virtue or a vice, he maintains of any agent: "There is no compulsion on him nor is there any external cause which makes him incline toward a virtue or a vice, except for his being disposed by temperament so that something is easy or difficult for him—as we have explained. There is no way at all that he is forced or hindered."[10] He has a reason for insisting on this that was not a reason for Aristotle, namely: "If man's actions were done under compulsion, the commandments and prohibitions of the Law would be nullified and they would all be absolutely in vain, since man would have no choice in what he does."[11] It is, according to Maimonides, only because "all of man's actions are given over to him"[12] that "there can be instruction and learning, as well as everything that involves instruction in, and habituation to, the laws."[13] For our purposes, the point here is not that moral requirements are revealed (though, of course, for *him*, that was of the first importance) but that we find here a different interpretation of the relation between ethical requirements and the ability to fulfill them. It is a version of 'ought implies can.' There are objective moral requirements, and we must be able to grasp what they are and respond to them. Accordingly, the power of the will that Maimonides ascribes to human agents is wider than the sort of character-shaping voluntariness we find in Aristotle. Even the agent who is established in certain patterns of judgment, desire, and reaction can act in a way incongruent with those patterns and can acquire different patterns. No one's record of action and feeling forecloses on departing from that record, for better or for worse.

We should observe that Maimonides does not recognize practical wisdom as a virtue in the way that Aristotle does, and this is almost certainly because of the role that revealed law plays in his view. (There are other reasons as well concerning Maimonides' strongly intellectualist conception of perfection. To pursue those differences here would take us too far afield.) On Maimonides' view, moral requirements are not out of reach, even to the bad man. Even if an agent lacks good judgment and good habits, what he should do is accessible to him in a way that is not part of Aristotle's account because the Law is known. "The Law specifies what actions are obligatory regarding all sorts of matters that for the Aristotelian gentleman would be subject to the deliberation of practical wisdom."[14] There is scope for interpretation, elaboration, and dispute about how laws apply to particular cases. In the tradition to which Maimonides belongs there is ample scope for dialectic, development, and dispute. He does not advocate any sort of blind obedience to divine law. He advocates the study of it so that through our understanding we come to love its wisdom and act accordingly. Still, the Law is a code of ethical requirements within the boundaries of which all of this is to take place. It is the set of rules and the standard by which one can recognize the moral quality of certain desires or passions and the actions that they might motivate. It enables us to have a kind of practical knowledge and self-knowledge that we would lack in its absence. There is an accessible, authoritative resource for understanding the ethical significance of our dispositions and actions.

In that respect, Maimonides' understanding of objectivity is more like what is found in many non-Aristotelian theories, even when they are not shaped by religious considerations. It is, for example, more like Kant's view than like Aristotle's. Maimonides and Kant have dramatically different views of the source of moral law, but both maintain that the mature agent's character is not an insurmountable barrier to the agent recognizing what virtue requires and to the agent's will effectively turning toward virtue. For Maimonides, of course, it is not our own reason which is the source of the moral law. Still, in contrast to Aristotle, both Maimonides and Kant maintain that an agent is capable of knowledge of ethical requirements and capable of an effective volition to alter his practical dispositions.

MORAL LAW, SECOND NATURE, AND ETHICAL SELF-CORRECTION

In the Maimonidean view, the Law supplies not just rules that guide action and specify requirements and prohibition but also corrective measures that *restore* the soul. There are strategies for ethical self-correction in addition to the requirements for virtue. "*The Law of the Lord is perfect, making wise the simple, restoring the soul.*"[15] (italics in original) Obedience to the Law is a strategy of moral retrieval and not just a guide to virtue for those who already aspire to it. "If we were convinced that we could never make our crooked ways straight, we should forever continue in our errors, and perhaps add other sins since we did not see that any remedy was left to us."[16] The moral law includes prescriptions for reform of character, and our volitional capacities are adequate to make those reforms. The enlarged power of the will found in Maimonides' account is necessary to re-engage ethically disordered agents to moral requirements. And the change that repentance brings about is a change brought about by the repentant agent not by supernatural causality. For the Law's effectiveness as a guide to perfection, it is necessary that agents can do what it requires and can reconnect with requirements even if they have a pattern of ethical lapse or straying.

It would be easy (and it has often been done) to interpret this sort of view as rendering virtue largely a matter of legalistic compliance. However, Maimonides' primary concern is the condition of the agent's soul. Meeting the requirements of the Law is a strategy of perfection. What can appear to be tedious detail with respect to practical requirement is meant as an elaboration of strategies of excellence and also redemption, obedience to which ethically perfects us. The relevant change is not merely behavioral. It is one thing to apologize for this or that particular action, but the project of repentance is a quite different undertaking. It is attachment to different values, and, correspondingly, a change in the agent's dispositions. Maimonides says a great deal about specific types of acts that are wrong and about what sort of repentance is proper to each, and he not only acknowledges the difficulty of the task, but, like Aristotle, he is mainly interested in the characteristics one's actions tend to establish and express.

It may be that for many commandments the rationale is not at all clear, and many commandments may seem to be irrelevant to contemporary circumstances (in his time, no less in ours).[17] He confronts the issue of how irrelevant or obsolete many commandments seem. This is an issue especially in regard to ritual laws. His response is that even when we do not clearly understand the rationale of a law, or when the original rationale seems to be no longer relevant, there is an ethically significant point in observing the law as part of the discipline of virtue leading to knowledge of the good. It is part of the discipline that enables perfection.[18] In a more secularized version of his point, we might say that agents who are being habituated in virtue or who aspire to it will often not understand the point of many requirements. They will not see their relevance or appreciate how acting in *those* ways conduces to virtuous states of character. That is, they need to be habituated to recognize the 'that' before they understand the 'because.' Indeed, they may never understand the 'because.'

The process of repentance and self-correction works through the agent altering his own dispositions by an effort of will until the ethically unsound dispositions are undone and replaced by more sound ones. That is a task the agent has the capability to perform, given the power of volition. There is plasticity in character because of that volitional power, and even long-established dispositions can be effectively renounced and replaced. In this view, the vicious person does have other "moves to make." (This was Broadie's expression.) The agent with a concern to improve his character can find another way of doing things which, if followed, will lead to *another way of seeing things*. It is important that there should be other moves to make because repentance and reform of character are typically so hard. An agent may believe that he is not who he should be, that at least some of his valuative attachments are shallow or misguided, and that it is increasingly painful to just go on in the way he is accustomed to going on. It does not follow that he has attained any effective clarity about where he should go or effective clarity about how to get there. On the Maimonidean view there is the needed clarity and also the power of will to effectively turn in that direction. The interest in self-correction will remain merely aspiration without real practical efficacy in the absence of both the cognitive and volitional capacities to engage in the task. What the view shares with many secular views is that ethics is largely a matter of law (or principle), and that rational agents as such are able to ascertain what the law requires and to enact those requirements. Moreover, rationality is also often supposed to be a capacity that enables agents to ethically recompose themselves, even if they are long-established in vicious dispositions.

In the attempt to change, agents may energetically undertake some new discipline or regime or seek a change of setting in order to eliminate certain temptations. This would be only part of the process. The relevant kind of reform of character is not just the discipline of not doing *that* again (with some specific type of wrong act in mind). It involves the undoing of certain motivational tendencies and also changes in attitudes and judgment, none of which is effected simply by decision. Antony Duff writes: "A sincere repentance of my wrong-doing involves a sincere desire to reform myself. I recognise and am distressed by the harm which I have done to others. I see that I have harmed myself, by injuring my relationships with others—by separating myself from God or the Good; from those whom I have directly wronged; from other members of the community whose values I have betrayed; and from myself as someone who truly desires good rather than evil."[19] This would be a change in the agent's fundamental and effective conception of what is practically necessary, of what he "has to" do, and a change in his willingness to do it.

Even in a moral philosophy which rejects the present account of ethical disability there should be an acknowledgment that character change of that type is such that the momentum of second nature generally runs strongly against it. Still, a point in favor of plasticity is that people do sometimes seem to really change, giving up their ways and adopting new ones. We sometimes say that our conscience will not let us go on in the accustomed way and that we cannot live with ourselves unless we make real and enduring changes in what we value and what we do. Also, there seems to be plasticity in the direction of worsening, as in the agent who changes by becoming mean, suspicious, and manipulative on account of resentment and disappointment, for example. Overall, though, character is often remarkably conservative even through change in belief and experience. For example, in many cases of worsening, what seems to be shown is that what we took to be virtues of the agent were not in fact firmly established as second nature and that this agent's behavior and attitudes are particularly sensitive to fortune. What looked like strengths were really just features of character that had not been tested. Maybe when this agent's moral luck runs out, his virtue runs out with it. Also, what looks like repentance or reform of character is often really just an acknowledgment that one has vices or undesirable characteristics but without undoing or overcoming them. Perhaps efforts at change initially appear to be sincere and efficacious, and indeed for a time they are, but over time the agent's 'true' character prevails. This is distressingly familiar.

One of the reasons it is so difficult to bring about changes in our characters is that habit is pleasing, even habits we are not glad to have. "Thus even when some aspect of a way of life proves detrimental to the person living that life, that person will find it difficult to relinquish even undesirable character traits if they help sustain a settled existence."[20] In addition, what is second nature to us is often pleasing just on account of its being a disposition we act from easily. "Habits also are pleasant; for as soon as a thing has become habitual, it is virtually natural" (*Rhetoric* 1370a6–7). We may realize that acting or reacting in a certain way, such as getting angry too quickly, or being too self-centered, is something we should change, but change can be painful. It is work, and there is comfort in the familiar, even if by our own standards it is not admirable. Or, we may feel that our identity is so bound up with a certain characteristic that even if we realize that it is not admirable, we are loath to disown it and to try to acquire a different characteristic. To do so would be to give up a part of ourselves, and we find that threatening.

Change in mature character involves overcoming dispositions formed by one's own voluntary activity. Maturing is difficult, but genuine character change can be much harder. This is one reason why habituation is so crucial. In the process of maturing we need to make judgments and commitments about what sort of person to try to become. We might recognize ourselves as having certain tendencies or susceptibilities and also recognize that it is not good to have them. In the case of trying to change mature character, in contrast to the case of how we habituate ourselves in the process of maturing, we are up against voluntary habits and tendencies which we already have a history of finding pleasing, and in which we have invested ourselves. We are also up against ourselves in the sense that our own voluntariness has had a role in our becoming like that. Our own policies of choice and motivation have shaped our dispositions. Genuine reform of character in the direction of virtue would require the agent's recognition of values that have not been his own. Yet, if a person is long-established in a second nature, it may be especially difficult to bring those values into view. Punishment *may* have some efficacy in that direction, prompting the agent to acknowledge as wrong some value(s) that she has been committed to. On the other hand, it may be an experience that embitters the agent and exacerbates her alienation from those values because the agent may not see her wrong as a lapse from a correct standard.

An agent may 'go through the motions' of some sort of regime of repentance (apology, self-effacing remarks, etc.) or perform acts of 'compensatory' virtue, but merely as a way of 'balancing the account' and not as part of really changing the way she goes about her leading her life. Often, people will exert themselves much more energetically in the effort to restore others' good opinion of them or to secure forgiveness than they will in making the changes in themselves that would merit a restoration of respect and trust and so forth. They may see the need to make changes and will make gestures in the right directions but may not be willing or able to genuinely commit to different conceptions of how to act and to the task of acting in those ways. Again, an important part of the explanation may be that we often strongly identify with certain of our characteristics, so that to change them, even thinking that we should, is especially difficult because of the way in which it would seem to call into question our identity.

It is the ethically disabled agent, the agent persistently and significantly alienated from good, with whom we are primarily concerned. In the case of that sort of agent the alienation need not bring with it the phenomenology of alienation, so that person's task is much more difficult and unlikely to succeed. Of the phenomenological issue Herbert Morris writes: "It is a moral good, then, that one feel contrite, that one feel the guilt that is appropriate to one's wrongdoing, that one be repentant, that one be self-forgiving and that one have reinforced one's conception of oneself as a responsible being."[21] The aim of repentance and punishment in his view, is to promote "one's general character as a morally autonomous individual attached to the good."[22] It is just this sort of attachment to and concern for moral good from which the ethically disabled agent may be cognitively and motivationally alienated. It is not just self-love or worries about one's identity that are in the way of self-correction. Habits entrenched as second nature may prevent the agent from bringing moral good into view and from caring that she fails to do so. The goods that Morris identifies are indeed goods, yet the vicious agent may not be susceptible to responding to the reasons that they are goods and may not care to enjoy them. So, just those agents who would gain most from contrition, repentance, and self-forgiving may be most remote from having an interest in undertaking them. They do not have in themselves the needed resources of understanding or motivation, and they do not know who to take as examples of virtue.

LAW AND LIVING NORMS

In accord with the contrasts between Maimonides and Aristotle that we have noted so far, there is in Maimonides an emphasis on self-examination. He writes: "Similarly, the perfect man needs to inspect his moral habits continually, weigh his actions, and reflect upon the state of his soul every single day. Whenever he sees his soul inclining toward one of the extremes, he should rush to cure it and not let the evil state become established by the repetition of a bad action—as we have mentioned."[23] This sort of self-consciousness is somewhat foreign to Aristotle's account of the agent, and, in particular, the idea that the "perfect man" should be especially self-conscious with respect to character is, in certain respects, un-Aristotelian. This sounds more like the kind of moral self-examination that Kant prescribes when he writes: "The command is: know (scrutinize, fathom) yourself, not in terms of your natural perfection (your fitness or unfitness for realizing all your arbitrary and obligatory ends), but rather in terms of your moral perfection, in relation to your duty. Know your heart—whether it is good or evil, whether the source of your actions is pure or impure. Know what can be imputed to you and what belongs to your moral state, whether as something inherent in man's substance or as something derived (acquired or admitted [into his being])."[24] The requirement to know not only one's duties but also one's moral state is found in a number of variants throughout moral philosophy. In certain respects, Smith's impartial spectator is an example and so too are theories in which conscience has an explicit role. The import of this is not just the emphasis it puts on motive but on the agent making an honest appraisal of the moral quality of his acts. It is unsurprising that this should be an important feature of moral theories which give a place to divine commands and God for whom there are no secrets and also to theories (though not all; utilitarianism is arguably an exception) in which there are fundamental principles or criteria of right action.

It is not that Aristotle pays no attention to self-regard or to what are the appropriate attitudes toward one's self. His lengthy discussion of self-love, for example, is a consideration of the propriety and importance of certain forms of self-regard. His discussion of the virtues generally is sensitive to the ways in which characteristics both reflect and are grounds for various types of self-regard. For example, he says: "We must also examine what we ourselves drift into easily. For different people have different natural tendencies towards different goals, and we shall come to know our own tendencies from the pleasure or pain that arises in us. We must drag ourselves off in the contrary direction; for if we pull far away from error, as they do in straightening bent wood, we shall reach the intermediate condition" (*NE* 1109b1–7). Aristotle's acknowledgment of individuality is certainly indicative of a role for self-awareness and monitoring one's actions and habits with a view to bringing them into the mean. In addition, he very plausibly observes that part of the importance of friendship is that through it we are able to achieve a better perspective on ourselves. "We are able to observe our neighbors more than ourselves, and to observe their actions more than our own" (*NE* 1169b35). Through our friends' responses to us and through their counsel and their care we enlarge our perception of our own character and human good. Aristotle is certainly not indifferent to self-awareness and the importance of truthful self-assessment. There is nothing mechanical or thoughtlessly automatic about the virtuous agent's judgments and reactions.

Maimonides, however, is talking about an intensive, ongoing, morally sensitive project of self-monitoring which he takes to be part of adult moral responsibility, even for the virtuous. It is the fixed reference of the moral law that makes such self-monitoring possible. There is a counterpart to this in non-theistic ethical theories wherein the scrutiny of one's conscience or the rigorous application of reason can reveal one's ethical shortcomings or misunderstandings. Part of the point of identifying ethical disability is to indicate that we may need to reconcile ourselves to limits on the efficacy of those capacities. The power of self-examination to reveal our moral characters and to effectively motivate and orient efforts at improvement in them depends upon the characters that do the looking and the sort of valuative interest they can take in what they find. That is perhaps obvious. Neither divine commands nor fundamental principles of practical reason on their own can make people look honestly at themselves. But it makes a difference whether self-scrutiny can be expected to have effective guidance.

A difference between an ethic of codifiable objectivity and an ethic of practical wisdom is that, in the former, there are specifiable criteria about who is an example of ethical excellence even when agents lack virtue. The Law (or reason, or the impartial spectator, or reflection behind the veil of ignorance) makes it possible to ascertain who are excellent individuals and makes it possible for us to judge ourselves by those criteria. In one way or another, this notion that the criterion of right action or the standards of excellence or virtue are accessible to all rational agents is a common feature of many moral theories. To some extent, the notion of a standard is reflected in Aristotle's view that the excellent agent is a living norm. (See, for example, *NE* 1113a25–35, 1144a30–35, 1176a10–20). The judgment of the *phronimos* is not determinative of good; the virtuous agent has sound ethical cognition, a correct understanding of good. His judgment does not constitute practical truth, though it is a reliable guide to it. However, excellent judgment is not formulable in a system of codifiable requirements that can be presented in the form of a theory or that can be derived from a criterion or fundamental principle. This is why the example of the *phronimos* and habituation are so crucial.

Maimonides too recognizes the significance of examples to emulate, and he puts weight on the importance of being influenced by the excellent. There is, of course, no mutual exclusion between the notion of a living norm and the notion that there are formulable standards of right or virtue. And in the business of living and learning what is good, that there are accessible, codified requirements does not displace the role or significance of living norms. Study of the Law needs to be complemented by our following the wise in their way of life and not just in their knowledge of law and legal opinion. He says: "It is natural to be influenced, in sentiments and conduct, by one's neighbors and associates, and observe the customs of one's fellow citizens. Hence, a person ought constantly to associate with the righteous and frequent the company of the wise, so as to learn from their practices, and shun the wicked who are benighted, so as not to be corrupted by their example."[25] And, "It is an affirmative precept to attach oneself to sages and their disciples, so as to learn from their example."[26] Also, for Maimonides the members of the covenanted community have a crucial role to play in the teaching of the Law and in upholding standards of ethical excellence. The teaching of the Law is a crucial part of the life of that community. The criteria need to be employed in governing the process of habituation. There is, though, a combined emphasis on self-awareness and the requirement to aspire to ethical perfection along with the specification of those standards that is fundamental to this conception of ethics. Living norms are crucial, but we can know who they are because of the Law, because of the codification of objective requirements.

We should be careful, however, not to overstate the extent to which the lack of codifiability confines an agent to the resources of his own practical reason. After all, in the present account we have put a great deal of weight on habituation. Also, with Aristotle we should acknowledge not only the importance of habituation but also that one's relations with others and one's participation in the pursuit of the overall welfare of the community are crucial to the acquisition of virtue. He says: "But it is hard for someone to be trained correctly for virtue from his youth if he has not been brought up under correct laws, since the many, especially the young, do not find it pleasant to live in a temperate and resistant way. Hence laws must prescribe their upbringing and practices; for they will not find these things painful when they get used to them" (*NE* 1179b32–35). The individual who is striving to be virtuous is not isolated, with his resources of ethical guidance limited to his own understanding and perception. The context for both the acquisition and the exercise of the virtues involves all of the complexity of political life, from relations in the family, to relations with friends, to the wider relations of many kinds with other members of the community and participation in its institutions.[27] The difference between Aristotle and Maimonides is not over whether there is a role for social life (family, friends, law, and the community in general) in the acquisition of virtue, but over the source, character, and accessibility of the guides to excellence, and, consequently, over the role of character in ethical cognition. This is indicative of a centrally important difference in ethical theorizing, one that makes possible the explanation of real practical possibilities for people (and correspondingly, reasonable expectations of them).

REASONS TO HESITATE IN ASCRIBING DISABILITY

I remarked earlier that we often cannot know if an agent is incorrigible, because we cannot be certain if that person's character is fixed. Indeed, we often do not know in our *own* cases at what point a disposition settles into fixity, though we know that like activities cause like characteristics. There are epistemic barriers to fully confident, indefeasible judgments that an agent's character is fixed. This may be the case even if it is incontrovertible that the agent has done something very terrible or has done many such things. There is also a *moral* reason to take seriously the possibility of character change on the part of the persistently vicious. A judgment that someone is incorrigible is often hard to keep separate from the judgment that that person is worthless, and that can dangerously corrupt our regard for that person. We might be more willing to forgive or to respond constructively, or at least be more slow in settling into contempt or hatred, if we believe that the wrongdoer might meaningfully acknowledge her wrong. The judgment that an agent is ethically disabled should be a last resort with regard to any agent who is not constitutionally disabled or insane. The fact that retributive sentiments may be quite clearly merited does not mean that there are no other kinds of ethically relevant responses that are also appropriate. I have argued that retributivism is not as vulnerable to objections as it is often claimed to be, but that does not exclude other kinds of considerations from having merit and weight. The epistemological consideration gives reinforcement to the moral one. We cannot be certain whether the agent is incorrigible and that her wrong acts reflect a deep, abiding viciousness. At the same time, we need to exercise great caution in not letting undisciplined retributive sentiments "lead us." [28]

We might observe also that sometimes agents who may seem to be deeply and persistently vicious or incorrigible may be in a state of denial concerning their own ethical understanding and ability to see things and act differently. People will 'dig in' out of defensiveness and refuse to acknowledge their wrong or their defects of character because doing so would be a blow to self-esteem. They will try to 'tough it out' and would rather be accused of wrongdoing than admit that they could have acted better and that they know how seriously they have erred. They will claim that they do not feel regret, they will say they would do it again, and the like, but more out of pride than sincerity. It is easier (sometimes, in some ways) to insist that one was not wrong in having done something quite awful than to admit that one knew better or could have acted differently. Here is one way that self-love misrepresents and distorts our understanding and self-knowledge in an especially unhelpful manner. This agent is still reachable.

Given the difficulty of these judgments of agents, including ourselves, even the strong 'fixity' view does not counsel ethical abandonment, either with respect to ourselves or others. [29] There is a powerful combination of ethical and epistemological reasons why no one should be simply 'written off' as incorrigible. It would be both a wrong done to the guilty agent and a worsening of us to morally abandon agents. However, there may not be a corresponding confidence that the agent does indeed have the capacity for reform or even for the acknowledgment of the need to change. Our ethical reasons for not lowering someone's status as a participant in the ethical order may not be evidentially supported by what we know about that person. A person does not have to earn that status in order to possess it, but there are numerous examples of individuals' actions that seem to compromise that status.

In any event, the main claim is not that character always becomes so fixed that it is impossible to change. Rather, the point is that even agents who are voluntary, responsible agents not lacking capacities of practical reason may be up against considerable obstacles to reforming their characters. The combination of natural, human tendencies to rationalize and to seek consoling explanations and self-deceptions, along with the absence of a codified morality including prescriptions for reform, makes for a considerable obstacle to ethically significant character change for the better. Thus, even if the claims for fixity are not necessary truths, they alter the moral landscape and the prospects and possibilities to be found there. There may be moral agents who stubbornly resist the most generous and resolute efforts to get them to see ethical sense, and, in that way, those agents are ethically disabled. They are steadfastly unrepentant and unregenerate, even though they are not out of their minds. They are not outside the boundaries of those who are full-fledged participants in the ethical world. Our relations with them are especially difficult because normative considerations that apply to them do not carry weight with them. But their lack of responsiveness does not deflect the bearing of those normative considerations on them.

The discussion of the issue of character change has presupposed that there are objective ethical considerations, and that there are virtues that it is objectively good for human beings to have. In the view that ethical ideals and commitments are best understood as domesticated to subjective projects or are relativized, there could still be considerable interest and importance with respect to the issue of character change, but that interest will not be related to the sorts of concerns about accessibility that I believe are real concerns. The metaethical discussion of chapter 5 will reinforce this point with a defense of realism. If there are objective values and objective human ethical excellences, then there is an especially important connection between character change and self-correction. There are objective ideals of excellence to aspire to even though the ethically disabled agent may find it impossible to bring them into view, no less realize them.

There is not a *necessary* connection between the metaethics and the moral psychology, but there is an *important* connection. Our views about the nature and acquisition of virtue and about the fixity of character go together in a way that plausibly relates the objectivity of ethical considerations to the fact that they are inaccessible to some agents. The inability of the ethically disabled agent to overcome that condition is not exclusively a matter of bad constitutive luck. It is something the agent has brought about and for which the agent bears ongoing responsibility.

The moral psychology of many modern moral theories involves a kind of democratic rationalism that we have called into question. Theistic moral theories too, involve their own sort of optimistic democracy through the theology of grace, through revelation and salvation. No one is hopelessly cut off from the good. If theism is true, then grace can do what reason and nature cannot do and can make possible the ethical redemption of any agent. But if moral psychology and ethics are not aided by grace, then there could be ethically disabled agents who are not straightforwardly psychopathic or who are less than full-fledged responsible agents. This is the view that is supported by the most plausible naturalistic ethic and moral psychology. The role of voluntariness in the formation of character and the role of character in ethical cognition lend considerable support to the view, though there are other considerations, such as the role of *conscience,* which demand further exploration.

CHAPTER 4

Conscience and Its Work

Are there any features of rational agency that we have neglected that might answer our doubts about whether 'ought' implies 'can' and our doubts about whether agents typically can 'know better'? Are the good offices of conscience adequate to those tasks? We will see that the answer is no, or at least that the claim that they are adequate needs to be qualified in significant ways. Conscience merits discussion though, because of the attributes that have been assigned to it and their relevance to the concerns of this account.

The notion of conscience connects various aspects of moral personality and has been regarded as a faculty by which we ascertain moral requirements. Conscience has also been held to have a motivational role; it supplies a motivational basis for acting rightly, and it is binding, and has been held to be the basis of proper feelings of remorse and practices such as repentance. I hope to show that notions of the authority of conscience, its practical necessity, and its motivational role can be explained in terms of the second natures of agents without identification of any distinct cognitive or motivational capacity or power which every agent has. The phenomena referred to in the idiom of 'conscience' are indeed important, but their explanation does not require a distinctive faculty or capacity that can effectively connect us to true values and enable moral self-correction even if we are ethically disabled. Here again we find that moral philosophy exhibits an optimism which moral psychology may disappoint. We will start on our way toward these results by briefly considering some of the main views of conscience.

THE VARIOUS CONCEPTIONS OF CONSCIENCE

In some views conscience is taken to have cognitive authority in the sense that conscience ascertains what it is we are to do. Sometimes it is understood to be verdictive, in that it judges our acts and conscience 'tells' us whether we have acted rightly or wrongly, and imposes a penalty if we have acted wrongly. If we have done so we feel the pain of remorse or shame, the sting of conscience. Another important function often assigned to conscience is to reconnect the agent to true values. The wrongdoer who is remorseful and sees the need for a project of correcting his values or motivations is responding to his conscience. We might say that conscience condemns the wrong act, presents the need for a penitential response, and directs the process of reform. It is also widely held that each person *has* a conscience, or at least that it is extraordinary and disturbing if a person does not. Everyone, it is widely held, has some sense of morals, some sense of what is right and what is wrong. An agent without conscience is hardly recognizable as a participant in the moral world. To criticize someone for being a coward or for being a liar is bad enough, but to ask of someone "have you no conscience?" is often tantamount to asking if the person is insane or thoroughly evil.

Moreover, in claiming to be motivated by conscience one is claiming that it was not just desire or self-interest that rationalized the act; the motive was grounded in the sense of what is most important, in the most fundamental sense of what is required. This points to another aspect of conscience. It is often taken to be deeply personal, and in heeding conscience an agent is responding to an imperative or a demand that is grounded in, or comes from, himself.[1] Alternatively, the authoritative aspect has also been interpreted as connecting conscience to objective moral considerations, rationally necessary principles, or to divine command. And, of course, all of these aspects of conscience are found in various combinations. However much diversity there is in the idiom of conscience, there is the presumption that it must be referring to some significant features of moral life and moral phenomenology.

Philosophers have tended to emphasize one or another of the authoritative, verdictive, sanctioning, and motivational aspects. Sometimes they conjoin two or more, but they typically take one of them to be focal. Butler, for example, joins the authoritative (which he takes to be cognitive) and the verdictive. He writes: "There is a superior principle of reflection or conscience in every man which distinguishes between the internal principles of his heart, as well as his external actions; which passes judgement upon himself and them, pronounces determinately some actions to be in themselves just, right, good, others to be in themselves evil, wrong, unjust;

which without being consulted, without being advised with, magisterially exerts itself, and approves or condemns him, the doer of them, accordingly."[2]

Butler says of man that "He hath the rule of right within: what is wanting is only that he honestly attend to it."[3] He goes on: "Yet let any plain honest man, before he engages in any course of action, ask himself, Is this I am going about right, or is it wrong? Is it good, or is it evil? I do not in the least doubt but that this question would be answered agreeably to truth and virtue, by almost any fair man in almost any circumstance."[4]

Kant's account is weighted to the verdictive role. It is not, in his view, conscience which ascertains what we are to do; "The understanding, not conscience, judges whether an action is really right or wrong."[5] "Rather, reason here judges itself, as to whether it has really undertaken that appraisal of actions (as to whether they are right or wrong) with all diligence, and it calls the man himself to witness for or against himself whether this diligent appraisal did or did not take place."[6] In *Lectures on Ethics* he says, "conscience has the power to summon us against our will before the judgment-seat to be judged on account of the righteousness or unrighteousness of our actions."[7] In *The Doctrine of Virtue* he says, "conscience is an inner court in man,"[8] and: "Every man has a conscience and finds himself watched, threatened, and, in general, kept in an attitude of respect (of esteem coupled with fear) by an inner judge; and this power watching over the law in him is not something that he himself (arbitrarily) makes, but something incorporated in his being."[9]

Kant shares with Butler the view that of course each agent has a conscience, that conscience is not something one might or might not acquire. Butler's view of this is clear in the passage above. Kant says "conscience cannot be acquired and we have no duty to acquire a conscience: every man, as a moral being, has a conscience inherent in him."[10] He continues, "And when we say: this man has no conscience, what we mean is: he pays no attention to its verdict."[11]

Mill argues that conscience is the "internal sanction of duty"[12] rather than a faculty for ascertaining what is to be done. "Its binding force, however, consists in the existence of a mass of feeling which must be broken through in order to do what violates our standard of right, and which, if we nevertheless violate that standard, will probably have to be encountered afterwards in the form of remorse."[13] This feeling, which is "the essence of conscience",[14] is "a pain, more or less intense, attendant on violation of duty, which in properly cultivated moral natures rises, in the more serious cases, into shrinking from it as an impossibility."[15] He goes on to state that while "the moral feelings are not innate but acquired, they are not for that reason the less natural."[16] Also, Mill allows that "this sanction has no binding efficacy on those who do not possess the feelings it appeals to."[17]

Adam Smith's conception of conscience involves a number of the different aspects that have been identified. He describes conscience as the "supposed impartial and well-informed spectator . . . the man within the breast, the great judge and arbiter"[18] of our conduct. It is also that by which we render verdicts on the ethical soundness of our actions and that by which we experience the pleasures of approval or the pain of disapprobation on account of our motives and actions. Similarly for Thomas Reid, who writes, "That conscience which is in every man's breast, is the law of God written in his heart, which he cannot disobey without acting unnaturally, and being self-condemned."[19] The first principles of morals, he argues, are "the immediate dictates of the moral faculty"[20] and are known to us through consulting conscience.

Aquinas gives yet another interpretation of conscience. It is to be understood in relation to *synderesis*, which is a disposition by which we grasp practical first principles. "*Synderesis* is said to be the law of our intellect because it is a habit containing the precepts of the natural law, which are the first principles of human action."[21] And "the precepts of the natural law are to the practical reason what the first principles of demonstration are to the speculative reason, because both are self-evident principles."[22] A conscience is the application of these general principles to particular cases. It is the job of conscience, as an act of reason, to determine what is to be done, by making specific determinations of what is required on the basis of the principles supplied by *synderesis*.

Aquinas held that *synderesis* is infallible and that "the common principles, the natural law, in its universal meaning, cannot in any way be blotted out from men's hearts."[23] Describing *synderesis* according to Aquinas, Donagan writes: "Everybody has some understanding of the principles of morality and, inasmuch as he has it, cannot be mistaken about them. In this sense, *synderesis* cannot err."[24] In commenting on whether ethical principles can be blotted out, Aquinas distinguishes between first principles and others and, "as to the other, i.e., the secondary precepts, the natural law can be blotted out from the human heart, either by evil persuasions, just as in speculative matters errors occur in respect of necessary conclusions; or by vicious customs and corrupt habits, as among some men, theft, and even unnatural vices, as the Apostle states (Rom. I. 24), were not esteemed sinful."[25]

In the Thomistic view conscience can err, because there can be errors of reasoning, but conscience is always to be obeyed. To fail to follow conscience would be to act on an intention not to do what one took to be morally required, and conscience is binding even when judgment errs.

On the basis of the preceding chapters, we can see that many traditional claims about conscience have had more weight placed upon them than they really can bear. If indeed agents can be ethically disabled in the way we have described, then there are voluntary, responsible agents who in important respects, lack conscience. Or, at least it cannot be expected that conscience will enable them to correct their valuative judgments and motivate them to ethically self-correct. This would also help explain why these agents do not regard their vicious actions as lapses from ethical standards. They see themselves as enacting true values.

As Mill recognized, and as our arguments so far suggest, there can be the phenomenology of internal sanction without it being engaged to true values. "Unhappily it is also susceptible, by a sufficient use of the external sanctions and of the force of early impressions, of being cultivated in almost any direction, so that there is hardly anything so absurd or so mischievous that it may not, by means of these influences, be made to act on the human mind with all the authority of conscience."[26] It is surely possible for an agent to identify with false values but to be conscientious in enacting them. For example, particularly devoted members of a gang or a ruthless organization may be rigorous in meeting the demands that they make upon themselves in upholding the values of the group. They are susceptible to self-reproach, shame, and self-doubt driven by those values, even if the values are perverse. The authority of conscience can be misplaced, and there is nothing about the very nature of conscience to preclude or prevent that.

With the influence of false religious ideas in particular, chiefly in mind, Adam Smith charitably observes: "There is still, however, something respectable in the character and behaviour of one who is thus betrayed into vice, by a wrong sense of duty, or by what is called an erroneous conscience. How fatally soever he may be misled by it, he is still, with the generous and humane, more the object of commiseration than of hatred or resentment. They lament the weakness of human nature, which exposes us to such unhappy delusions, even while we are most sincerely labouring after perfection, and endeavouring to act according to the best principle which can possibly direct us."[27] In this kind of case the "great inmate of the breast"[28] has obstructed vision, but the agent is still responding according to what he takes to be his duty. Conscience is at work in binding the agent to what he (mistakenly) takes to be true values.

In cases of that kind there might be a good deal of blurriness concerning blame. The agent knows what he is doing, is doing it because of what kind of action it is, but it is ethically perverse. There is no failure of agency of a sort that deflects blame, though the agent may been "betrayed into vice" by prevailing values and norms. Even though the agent consults his conscience he gets it wrong because of his attachments and dispositions. But this is to say that conscience will not reliably see past the perspectives established as second nature.

Earlier, in discussing practical necessity, we discriminated several different interpretations of "I have to." We might add to the list the 'have to' of conscience, as an awareness of moral obligation, perhaps with a special kind of bindingness. When we say, "My conscience required it," we mean not only that we recognize a requirement, but that failure to enact that requirement would be an especially serious matter for us as agents concerned with moral integrity. We also used the notion of 'silencing' to describe how, for the excellent agent, certain kinds of potentially action-guiding considerations are silenced, or nearly silenced. We could say that they are silenced by conscience. Yet that does not *further* explicate what silencing is. With respect to the person who experiences moral conflict, we can say that it is a struggle between conscience and other motives. Again, however, that does not further explicate the struggle or the resolution of it. Finally, in the persistently vicious or ethically disabled agent there could be the same phenomenological features of conscience, though the agent's values are false values.

THE OPERATIONS OF CONSCIENCE

There are still several acts and habits of practical responsibility to which 'conscience' aptly applies even in light of these criticisms of theories of it. Moreover, the ways in which we informally use the idiom of conscience outside of the context of theorizing reflect many of those theoretical claims. We say that an agent has a conscience in the sense that he has a measure of concern with whether or not his actions conform to his convictions. Also, conscience is at work when an agent has to resolve for himself whether to follow through with what he judges to be ethically required; perhaps it is his conscience that prods him to muster his courage when it is not his second nature to act in the way that courage here and now requires. Again, an agent's conscience is at work when he acknowledges his own defects and lapses, and this acknowledgment is painful and has motivational efficacy. We can imagine saying of the gossip who gives up the habit, "Well, he's got a conscience, after all." This agent now feels some guilt or shame about his previous actions, and these feelings are part of the process of connecting with values that disallow the practice. With respect to a child, we speak of conscience in terms of norms and rules that the child internalizes and which it is painful to the child to violate. The child does not yet have an understanding of what makes those norms and rules right ones (maybe they are not) but is habituated to feel badly for violating them. We can encourage in the child the development of awareness of the character and consequences of his actions so that even at an early age there is an acknowledgment that it matters what one does. In this way we encourage the development of conscience.

Conscience is also a concern to act on the basis of considerations other than narrowly self-interested ones and to learn from experience lessons that are not confined to the strictly prudential. Kant remarks that "we all have an impulse to flatter and blame ourselves in accordance with the rules of prudence."[29] This, he says, is "analogous" to conscience, and "men often mistake it for conscience."[30] In these cases it is not the wrongfulness of the act for which the agent reproaches himself, it is "for the imprudence which led to detection."[31] It is some prudential learning, not the ethical character of the act (or oneself) which is the issue for the agent. An active conscience would make clear the difference.

Not infrequently we will do something for what we claim are the right reasons, when in fact, other considerations are moving us. In some sense we might even know this, but we try to deceive ourselves all the same. Augustine, in the *Confessions* writes: "What I say I am doing and really desire to do for my health's sake, I do in fact for the sake of the enjoyment. For there happens not to be the same measure for both: what suffices for health is too little for enjoyment; so that often it is not at all clear whether it is the necessary care of my body calling for more nourishment, or the deceiving indulgence of greed wanting to be served. Because of this uncertainty my wretched soul is glad, and uses it as a cover and an excuse, rejoicing that it does not clearly appear what is sufficient for the needs of health, so that under the cloak of health it may shelter the business of pleasure."[32]

This sort of phenomenon is familiar enough. People often try to fool themselves because they want to think of themselves as acting in good conscience but at the same time they want to do that which conscience prohibits. In such cases it is not that we are incapable of a correct ethical realization, but *because* we are capable of it, and because it is incongruent with what we most want to do, we busy ourselves in keeping it out of view or in disguising it.

Another important type of case is where the agent goes ahead and acts with self-assurance, but when some feature of the act is brought into relief or is isolated, there is a sometimes stunning or stunned recognition of how wrong the act was. This is strikingly illustrated by the David and Nathan story in Second Samuel, chapters 11 and 12 in the Hebrew Bible. David wanted Uriah's wife, Bathsheba, for himself and ordered Uriah into the forefront of battle where he was sure to be killed, and, indeed, he was. The Lord sends the prophet Nathan to David, and Nathan tells the story of a rich man to whom a traveler comes. The rich man would not feed the traveler from his own flock and instead took a poor man's only, and beloved, lamb and prepared it for the traveler. David reacts with great anger and says that the rich man deserves to die, and that the poor man's loss should be restored to him fourfold. This is when Nathan says to him, "Thou art the man" and tells David of the evil that will befall his house because of his sin. David could already comprehend the values at stake in his treacherous dealing with Uriah but did not bother himself with their application to his own acts. He made the acknowledgment through his angry reaction to the injustice described in Nathan's story. He had to see the injustice in others before he could see it in himself.

In still another exercise of conscience, the realization of what was wrong in the act may only come much later. We think back upon something we did when young, which was perhaps quite hurtful to another, but it is only years later, as part of mature self-reflection, that we recognize and begin to feel strongly how wrong it was. Had our character developed differently, the episode might have been lost to ethical self-awareness, if not to memory as well. But we do see it now and appreciate its meaning with respect to how hurtful it was to the other person or how self-centered or inconsiderate it was. Just the fact that we did it, even though we would never consider doing anything like that *now* with adult awareness, can be enough for it to become a troubling focus of attention and concern. It is not that we should have known better when we did the thing; we were perhaps young enough to be excused on that score. Still, even though we were not blameworthy in full measure because of youth, conscience troubles us now. We now find it painful that we could have ever acted that way.

In spite of all of these perfectly apt uses of the notion of conscience, it is true that for a great deal of our ethical experience, conscience simply does not enter into it in any distinctive or self-conscious way. For one thing, much of the time, we engage in (and there is need to engage in) little if any explicit deliberation about what is required. Rather, our actions reflect our habits of attention, response, and so forth, and often that is sufficient. And even if we do deliberate, the content of the reasoning is likely to be an articulation and deployment of the habits of judgment and sensibility that are second nature. When our understanding does not seem adequate to a situation we try to make a discovery about what has ethical priority. We might call this an appeal to conscience, but it is not the activity of capacities other than the ordinary capacities of practical reason. Or, what we call 'conscience' may play a role when we are tempted by the appeal of something we judge to be wrong or base, but we cannot silence the appeal of it, as on the occasions of which we say, "Oh, I *wanted* to, believe me; but my conscience wouldn't let me."

There are occasions when extraordinary demands are made upon us or when we might say that it is conscience that enables us to recognize that these *are* extraordinary demands. Imagine the case in which the fugitive slave or the hunted but innocent refugee comes to your house. We sometimes find that our accustomed ways of carrying on and the sorts of justifications we give for them will not do. Someone with a conscience is someone who can see that customary practices or rationales are not adequate. Sometimes we believe we have to stand up for something or stand opposed to it because of what that something is and because of who we are or feel we must be. It is in such circumstances that people sometimes look or dig deeply into themselves and find resources of courage or resolve that they themselves may not have known were there. Even in these cases it is not conscience as a distinct, innate capacity that becomes operative. What moves and guides us is the result of reflection on our sense of who we are and what we must do to be who we think we should be. Earlier we noted that character sets limits, and that these can be strengths or defects. As Williams put it, "Incapacities can not only set limits to character and provide conditions of it, but can also partly constitute its substance."[33] They can be enabling limits or disabling limits. Conscience is not something else operating independently of those.

People sometimes sincerely acknowledge that there is some moral task of changing or recomposing themselves that they should undertake, and they are eager to prove that they can change. They may even seek out opportunities to be tested in order to prove to themselves and others that the change is real. This can be part of a process by which the agent changes his conception of what is practically necessary, what he has to do. Also, we sometimes sincerely acknowledge the justice of punishment, because we feel that we deserve it, and we think that only by undergoing the deserved punishment will our standing with ourselves and our relations with others be restored.

For the really excellent agent there may be little for conscience to do either by way of guiding action or guiding reflection about things one has already done. This agent has sound judgment, does not need prompting in order to act well, and does not need to exercise self-restraint in order to refrain from acting badly. Were the agent to fail to uphold his values he would feel guilt in a constructive way and would genuinely reaffirm the value in question. This agent's habits of perception, judgment, and decision effectively serve virtue without the agent needing to appeal to any sort of authority or principle in himself other than his habits of practical reason and the accompanying dispositions of sentiment.

On the other hand, there are plenty of agents whose ethical defects leave little effective role for conscience to play. When appeals to conscience are unavailing it is not always because the agent manages to inhibit or deflect what his conscience tells him. It may be that the agent's second nature is such that there just is no receptivity to the appeal. As a last stand for morality, we sometimes appeal to what we take to be some element of a common, fundamental grasp of moral limits or requirements. For example, the person who is considering selling her child for a supply of drugs (and who is not hopelessly, desperately addicted in such a way that she is plainly no longer a voluntary agent) is someone to whom we might say, "Look, no matter how bad it gets, no matter how much you want or need the drug, nothing is worth doing *that*." Just by being human she surely has some understanding of what is humanly important and some grasp of right and wrong. The same sort of appeal would be appropriate with respect to the supplier of the drugs waiting for the addict's decision: Who could be a party to that sort of exchange? Obviously, only very awful people, but there are such people.

Granted, the appeal to one's humanity often *is* the way to 'get through' to somebody and remind the agent of something that in some sense she already knows. We sometimes succeed in getting a person to finally and genuinely see what she ought to do, and we sometimes succeed in getting a person to see that she indeed can do what is required. We might attribute the success to the way conscience reminds us that there are some things such that it seems that no one could forgive herself for doing them. Yet, people do such things, and sometimes even feel no need to forgive themselves. They are just glad to have the drugs or the money or the child to illegally sell for adoption or worse. If an agent's character is bad enough to be ethically disabling, then it is not as though conscience will somehow escape intact and equip that agent with the capacity to engage with true values. The lack of effective conscience may not be a responsibility-defeating defect. To say an agent lacks conscience is sometimes just a way of describing ethical disability.

RESULTS OF THE DISCUSSION

The dispositions and capacities that bring ethical considerations properly into view are not grounded in an innate or constitutive faculty in anything like the way Butler, for example, describes. Even in theories such as Smith's, which do not treat conscience as innate or grounded in a priori reason or as a constitutive faculty there is a confidence about the reliability and efficacy of conscience that is overly optimistic. Moreover, a broadly Aristotelian moral psychology (correctly, I believe) focuses more on the agent's normative engagement with the world than on inner conflicts between obligation and inclination or egoism and altruism. There are such conflicts of course, but the moral psychology is not fundamentally shaped by those sorts of dualisms. When it is taken to be so shaped there is a more natural 'fit' for conscience in the way that Butler or Kant understood it. On such views, moral failing and weakness are to be diagnosed in terms of a conflict between some authoritative faculty or principle and other motives. There is conscience or reason or some grasp of moral principles which the sane, rational agent of course possesses, and there are the motives of self-interest, the passions, the desires that are to be organized, restrained or overridden by the exercise of the agent's moral capacities. The case that we have made so far should loosen the grip of this conception of ethical personality and its constitutive capacities by relocating in the second nature that an agent may or may not acquire, some of the features that are often located in primary nature.

It is not my aim to deflate or explain away the numerous ways in which conscience figures in our lives and in moral phenomenology. However, it would be a mistake to identify conscience as a faculty with certain powers, on the basis of *what an excellent person is like*. We should not conclude from the conception of an excellent agent that there is a constitutive capacity or faculty that is the source or ground of that excellence except when it is impeded in its operation. This is a kind of reading-back as an innate feature of human nature, something that agents can be habituated into. Acquired habits are essential to human excellence. An agent who fails to acquire good habits may just be an agent whose second nature is dominated by bad habits rather than an agent whose innate capacity for excellence is defective or absent. Here again, the lack of an ethical excellence (in this case, a well-formed and functioning conscience) is not evidence of the individual being less than fully an agent and a responsible agent. The innate capacity to acquire excellent habits is not the same as an innate tendency to excellence. In fact, there seem to be responsible agents who can hardly be said to have conscience at all. Conscience will not save a person from depravity or wickedness by 'intervening' from outside the agent's character. Like other ethically relevant dispositions, it must be practiced, and, like other ethically relevant dispositions, it cannot be fully isolated or compartmentalized. Regarding the person without conscience or the ethically disabled person as less than sane and less than a full-fledged, responsible participant in the ethical world is indicative of a denial of the involvement of the agent's voluntary investment as an agent in his viciousness.

In "The Moral Worth of Retribution" Michael Moore writes of how sometimes compassion for the victim of a crime gets transferred to the wrongdoer. He says, "My own view is that such a transfer of concern from victim to criminal occurs in large part because of our unwillingness to face our own revulsion at what was done. . . . It allows us to look away from the horror that another person was willing to cause."[34] Moore is making a case for the moral fitness of retributive sentiments, something we remarked on earlier, though it is not our main concern here. But his insight about the transfer of compassion comports with our view. I do think that often the willingness to regard people who do dreadful and deeply disturbing things as insane and thus not responsible (especially when they do them to other people, and not just to their property or other interests) is to some extent a psychological defense. It is how we distance ourselves from the reality that other people, who are not so different from us, not insane, or without rationality, can do such things. The basic defensive thought is "That's not *us*," or "That does not happen in the social and ethical world *we* are in." But it does.

Our willingness to assign these agents a status of 'non-responsible' or 'not sane' is also symptomatic of our own inability to make sense of how people could do the things that they do and be the sorts of people that they are. Often such agents seem to us to be people who, if they had had guidance or experiences of certain kinds at crucial times in their lives, would not have become so ethically disordered. As we have seen, even if this is true, it is not on its own a reason for regarding these agents as less responsible in some general way. We sometimes reconcile ourselves to this by diminishing them; no one who is a 'whole' person could be like that, so they must be less than 'whole'. Perhaps this is because we tend to think that people have some sort of natural inclination to the good, at least in the sense that they are naturally disposed to be responsive to considerations of good. I will say a bit about this below. Even though the fixity of the ethically disabled agent's dispositions limits his ability to act and respond differently from the way he does, he acts voluntarily in the relevant sense because the determination of his act by his character is determination of his act by *him*. We should not rush to infer that the agent who seems to have no conscience is less than sane, except in the sense that he loves or values the wrong things, and we cannot appreciate his reasons for what he does value and what he chooses to ignore.

ARE WE NATURALLY DISPOSED TO THE GOOD?

Ethically disabled agents are not renouncing the pursuit of good and are not renouncing rationality. The intelligibility of their action remains teleological in that end-oriented sense. These agents pursue false or perverse goods. This is not because of an absence of reason but on account of a disordered employment of it. Such agents have guiding conceptions of action and life and pursue them in a rational manner, though they are ethically unsound, and the agents are unbothered by that. These agents lack an active concern to act well and to have the dispositions to do so.

The disposition to pursue practical understanding and good does not operate independently of the agent's effort to operate it in a sound manner. In this respect it is similar to the disposition to seek knowledge that Aristotle refers to in the opening line of the *Metaphysics*, "All men by nature desire to know." (*Meta.* 980a22) Among other things, such as the general delight we take in gratifying curiosity, he is referring to the disposition which, when successfully exercised, causes and constitutes the completion or perfection of a human being. Still, even according to Aristotle's view, that disposition needs to be encouraged, actuated, and directed. The desire to know is natural in the sense that the fulfillment of it is a core perfection. Indeed, in his view, it is *the* core perfection of human nature, and he argues that the activity of understanding is naturally pleasing. The desire to know, however, is not a desire by which we are inevitably moved in a fully effective way. Similarly with practical normative thought, that is, with action-guiding valuative conceptions. Habit must actuate and direct the desire. Again, we can retain the understanding of action in teleological terms without that necessarily being hitched to either a comprehensive practical *telos* or to a typically effective tendency to realize human excellence.

Normativity is so thoroughly a part of our way of thinking about human beings that in spite of skepticism about an intrinsic end for human nature or objective moral considerations, it is widely thought that a thoroughly bad person is in some way defective as a human being. In modern philosophy, after the general repudiation and replacement of teleological metaphysics, we find statements such as the following, from Smith and Reid, respectively, concerning human beings. "Nature, accordingly, has endowed him, not only with a desire of being approved of, but with a desire of being what ought to be approved of; or of being what he himself approves of in other men."[35] And: "The intention of nature, in various active principles of man—in the desires of power, of knowledge, and of esteem, in the affection to children, to near relations, and to the communities to which we belong, in gratitude, in compassion, and even in resentment and emulation—is very obvious."[36] Even Hume writes, "It requires but very little knowledge of human affairs to perceive, that a sense of morals is a principle inherent in the soul, and one of the most powerful that enters into the composition."[37] (Though he does not mean this in the way Aquinas or Butler or Reid might interpret it.) To lack interest in the good or the right is indicative of a dubious claim to *rationality*. How could an agent be capable of reflectively assessing her desires, values, and actions, and have an awareness of the differences the latter make, and still persist in a way of life that causes needless suffering, that is indifferent to the welfare of others, or that is unjust or cruel? Moreover, how is it that this agent is not undone by internal conflict, or burdened by a painful awareness of the disordered state of her capacities?

Here again, we see that habituation is immensely important, for that is how conscience or concern for good, in whatever form it takes, is initially acquired and sustained. It is through habituation that an agent will acquire the practices of judgment and of self-evaluation that we recognize as exercises of conscience. Conscience does not operate, is not present, unless there is an interest in it, and that interest is not innate. It is an aspect of the developed interest one takes in the world as the object of practical concern. There is no specific form that it necessarily or naturally takes "on its own." It would be incorrect to say that human beings naturally actualize ethical good except when something stops them or misdirects them. A great deal has to go right and be done right in order for them to develop stable attachments to genuine goods. Independently of habit, convention, and the supporting fabric of contingent forms of social life human beings will not pursue virtue or develop conscience, and there is no guarantee that those contingencies will favor their development.

The role of these contingincies does not cast doubt on the claim that there are objective goods for human beings or that there are excellences that are perfections of human nature. However, these normative matters are not simply read off of the concept of rational agency or the concept of human nature, and are not elements of a single, unified *telos* for a human being. Our understanding of them emerges from reflection upon experience and ethical life. Our grasp of the reasons that certain goods are goods and our ability to appreciate them as such depend on second nature. Habituation is crucial to bringing a person into a condition to make these acknowledgments and to have these abiding concerns.

It is unsurprising that there is a role for conscience in theories of which moral considerations are interpreted as objective. 'Conscience' in such theories typically names our ability to grasp objective moral principles and to respond appropriately to their authority. But objectivity does not require that there be a realized capacity or a faculty in each agent that enables the effective grasp and appreciation of ethical considerations. It does not require that conscience be a constitutive feature of our nature. Especially where there are explicit theistic commitments or the influence of theological thought at work (as in Smith's and Reid's thinking, but not, for example, in Hume's or Mill's) conscience is likely to have a place, a role in constituting moral ethical personality by virtue of the stamp of the creator on human nature. Adam Smith describes moral principles as "the commands and laws of the Deity, promulgated by those vice-regents which he has thus set up within us"[38] And Reid writes, "our Moral Judgment or Conscience, grows to maturity from an imperceptible seed, planted by our Creator."[39] Though their theism is often regarded as not central to their moral philosophies, and the examination of the main elements of their moral epistemologies is now largely detached from their theism, it is clear that *they* did not take theism to be merely an accessory to their conceptions of human nature and morality. The present account has outlined some of the main elements of a naturalistic interpretation of ethics; one that does not help itself to the resources theism makes available. The naturalism is no threat to objectivity, but it does put certain important limits on what can be understood as basic, common, human capacities with respect to ethical matters.

In chapter 5 we will take up the issue of objectivity more directly and argue for a realist metaethic. A crucial element of the moral psychology presented so far is that the objectivity of ethical considerations does not ensure their accessibility, and this has important implications for understanding the way in which 'ought' and 'can' are related. As I indicated earlier, the account of ethical disability does not *essentially* depend on a realist metaethic, though I shall argue that ethical considerations are to be interpreted realistically and that moral psychology and a realist metaethic reinforce each other, as we will see.

CHAPTER 5

Metaethics and Moral Psychology

Although the discussion has proceeded with the presupposition that ethical considerations are objective, it must be granted that the moral psychological claims are consistent with different metaethical approaches. The account of ethical disability does not require a realist metaethic. Yet, there are relations of mutual support between the interpretations of those issues and realism, and they strengthen the case for them together. Looking at why this is so will further illuminate why the objectivity of ethical considerations is no guarantee of their accessibility. It will also help explicate the complementary roles of reason and sensibility in ethical cognition. Thus, the discussion of metaethics will elaborate our claims about the role of character in ethical cognition.

The main avenue of approach will be through examination of the debate between projectivism and realism. Recent work by Blackburn and McDowell will supply key reference points for those positions. That debate's formulation of the central issues is particularly apt for pursuing our main concerns here. It is not the project of this chapter to develop and present a full scale metaethical theory in its own right. The metaethical discussion is here in order to complement and elaborate our main claims about moral psychology. We begin with some observations about the recent history of metaethics in order to set the context.

SOME KEY FEATURES OF THE CURRENT DEBATE

Moore's critique of naturalism in the early twentieth century set an agenda for much of the subsequent metaethical debate. Many of his successors agreed that naturalism was untenable, but their approaches yielded sharply contrasting results concerning the correct interpretation of ethical value and ethical reasons. Antirealist, noncognitivist critics rightly put emphasis on the practical dimension of moral judgment and discourse, and they did so in a way that put pressure on intuitionism and cognitivism generally. The roles they assigned to the expression of sensibility and conative stances in moralizing raised fundamental questions about what realist values could be, how we could have knowledge of them, and how that knowledge could figure in ethical practice. Yet, the noncognitivism that emerged gave legitimate cause for wondering if a strategy that yielded *those* results could be the right strategy for giving an account of moralizing. It emphasized the prescriptivity and non-assertoric force of moral language but often seemed to disfigure moralizing to make it fit criteria motivated by other concerns. Instead of exploring the specific ethical roles of various emotions, reactive attitudes, desires, and conceptions of worth, these were generically lumped under headings such as 'pro-attitudes' (or the opposite), which hardly revealed the textures of the issues. Antirealist metaethics was often motivated by general theories of meaning and theories about the analysis of concepts that yielded results that could be deployed in metaethics, but the metaethical claims themselves seemed to be somewhat derivative. This is true of much of the antirealist critique of naturalism.

To some extent, prescriptivism recognized a larger role for rationality in ethical judgment. R. M. Hare's work gave more texture to the antirealist interpretation of moral discourse and reasoning than was found in some early versions of emotivism. In particular, the emphasis on universalization and consistency was a way to maintain rationality across a formal dimension while interpreting ethical judgment expressively. There still was not a role for ethical cognition, for ethical reason or comprehension, though there was a role for *reasoning* about ethical matters, since, given prescriptive premises, of course one could reason to conclusions about what to do, and the logic of those inferences was crucial.

In her critique of prescriptivism Philippa Foot argued that the sort of clean break between the descriptive and the evaluative that seemed to be taken for granted by both realist and antirealist critics of naturalism was not to be found. She developed a destructive critique of prescriptivism and a more positive account of ethical cognition as well as a moral psychology that was congenial to an approach that took the virtues seriously. Her arguments began to nudge the metaethical debate in the direction of concerns about ethical content and moral psychology, in contrast to more narrow attention to matters of ethical language.[1] "Modern Moral Philosophy" by G. E. M. Anscombe was another crucial source of arguments that raised fundamental concerns about the very conception of what moral philosophy is about and how it is to be done.[2] Anscombe and Foot (and others, such as Iris Murdoch) were drawing attention back to moral judgments and beliefs in their own right, so to speak, rather than arriving at results about them from some other area of conceptual or linguistic analysis.[3]

In the current debate, two of the most important approaches are sophisticated developments of some of the main concerns that figured in the Hare-Foot debates of the 1950s and 1960s. These are a Humean-Wittgensteinian antirealism (in various versions) and an Aristotelian-Wittgensteinian realism (in various versions). The Humeans tend to emphasize the dispensability of ontological commitments. The Aristotelians tend to emphasize the ways in which conative stances, responses, and valuations have a cognitive dimension that is not characterizable independently of their objects. The realist project is not an attempt to revive something like Moore's intuitionism but to show how judgment and reaction can be responsive to facts in ways that have full-fledged cognitive credentials. There is no attempt to diminish the role of sensibility. Indeed, an important part of the broadly Aristotelian project is to explicate the ways in which sensibility and understanding are inextricably connected in ethical judgment and in the acknowledgment of facts as ethically relevant considerations.

Both sides have drawn from the later work of Wittgenstein. His interpretations of rule-following and the use of concepts took concept-use and rationality generally to be normative matters. He argued that the correct ways of going on in the use of concepts are not codifiable in universal formulae, though we are not at a loss to distinguish correct from incorrect uses. Neither is knowing how to carry on correctly in the use of a concept entirely a matter of being in a certain specifiable psychological state. Or rather, no finite psychological state could explain what it is to grasp a rule for the use of a concept such that one can go on using it and understand it when others use it. There is the normativity of rule-following (the normativity of a term meaning the same on different occasions of use) involved in making the judgment, "The cows broke out of their enclosure" even though it is not a judgment concerning values. The Wittgensteinian insights about the normativity of rationality have been put to work by philosophers across a wide and diverse range, from linguistic idealists to realists, and they are centrally important to the views that will be discussed here.[4]

A lesson drawn via the Wittgensteinian influence by many antirealists is that there could be ethical judgment without an ontology of value, and that realism can be rejected without landing us in skepticism or person-relative subjectivism. We find this, for example, in the Humean-Wittgensteinian view of Blackburn. Specifically, this is not a skeptical view if a skeptical view both denies that values are objective or real and claims that because they are not, ethics is fundamentally undermined. Hume did not knock moral values off the pedestal of reality; he provided an account of moralizing (full-fledged moralizing) without an ontology of moral facts and without rational or intuitive insight into alleged moral facts or value-entities. For their part, some of the realists focus on how Wittgensteinian resources better enable us to explicate how moral judgments are cognitive and truth-evaluable *in spite of* there not being an ontology of value-entities and special faculties to perceive them. That is, the standard characterizations of realism and the exotica to which it is committed are misrepresentations. Also, in following Wittgenstein's lead into a closer examination of concepts in the actual judgments and contexts in which they are used, they have pursued the examination of specific moral concepts, rather than more global analyses of 'good' or 'right.' There is more diagnosis and exploration of the texture of specific concepts than attempts to locate principles or rules in a formally elaborated moral system based on a fundamental criterion of good or right.

Complementing this, some realists have 'officially' developed a more particularist account of ethical cognition. The particularism and antireductionism, along with the recasting of normativity, could be fitted into the project of rearticulating a virtue ethic in which the agent's sound appreciation of the ethical features of acts and situations replaced the teleology of actualizing human form. The virtues were favored because of the emphasis on specific types of receptivity and recognitional abilities and their role in judgment and motivating action. This is reflected in the non-Platonist, realist view developed by McDowell. The metaethic that is defended here is a virtue-centered realism of that general type.

Metaethics is another context in which the interpretation of *habits* is crucial, because the case for realism turns in large part upon the interpretation of the habits of thought involved in moralizing, and the extent to which they are cognitive habits. The case for antirealism correspondingly turns on a noncognitivist interpretation of habits of ethical thought. In order to see this, we will take a critical look at the merits of projectivism and consider why it can seem to be a credible alternative to realism, but in fact, is not. The habits of moral thought are indeed cognitive habits in a fuller sense than antirealism allows.

IS PROJECTIVISM ADEQUATE?

Projectivism is a development of some important strands of Hume's thought, modified by a restoration of some of the sophistication and complexity of it, which was not always in evidence in its emotivist and prescriptivist descendants. Projectivism takes up Hume's denial that there are value-entities and properties, and his denial that reason (or any other faculty) detects values. It also maintains Hume's stance that the basis of moral judgment and phenomenology lies in human affective propensities and that this explanation does not leave us with an impoverished morality. It was a mistake to think that morality needed a metaphysics and an epistemology of objective value. But the projectivist account is not driven by a positivist criterion of meaning; so despite the fact that it is basically expressivist, it is not thinly expressivist. It does not explain away what we take moralizing to be. It explains it, deploying broadly naturalistic resources.

One merit claimed on behalf of projectivism is that it avoids the kind of strain that might be detected between first-order belief and practice on the one hand, and an error-theoretic metaethic, on the other.[5] Error theory holds that common sense takes values to have primary-quality objectivity. However, the error-theorist's denial that this is the case is a premise for the conclusion that morality does not and cannot have the kind of objectivity and authority that common sense takes it to have. A projectivist metaethic purportedly does not disturb first-order practice or have skeptical consequences for it. Moralizing is not under-underwritten. Again, this is a sense in which it is Humean. The lack of rational warrant for ethical norms and judgments and the fact that they do not refer to moral facts or value-entities does not diminish moral judgment. We do not settle for something inferior to 'genuine' moral claims and disputes; we come to see all that moral claims and arguments are and can be. It appears to people that morality incurs a loss "only if a defective sensibility leads them to respect the wrong things."[6]

Blackburn says "It is because of our responses that we say that cruelty is wrong, but it is not because of them that it is so."[7] "What makes cruelty abhorrent is not that it offends us, but all those hideous things that make it do so."[8] His view is that "there is only one proper way to take the question 'On what does the wrongness of cruelty depend?': as a moral question, with an answer in which no mention of our actual responses properly figures. There would be an external reading if realism were true. For in that case there would be a fact, a state of affairs (the wrongness of cruelty) whose rise and fall and dependency on others could be charted. But antirealism acknowledges no such state of affairs, and no such issue of dependency."[9] He reinforces the view by noting that "if everyone comes to think of it as permissible to maltreat animals, this does nothing at all to make it permissible: it just means that everybody has deteriorated."[10] There is no question of looking at the wrongness of cruelty from a standpoint outside of ethics and trying to ascertain from there what facts make it wrong. With that, realism can agree. The central question is how to interpret the issue of how facts about cruelty count as ethically relevant, so that it can be shown that its wrongness indeed does not depend upon our actual responses. This is necessary in order to avoid the result that just any judgment of right and wrong is ethically in order.

Blackburn insists that giving up realism is costless, for: "The extra ingredients the realist adds (the values or obligations which, in addition to normal features of things, are cognized and the respect we then feel for these cognized qualities) are pulling no explanatory weight: they just sit on top of the story that tells how our sentiments relate to natural features of things."[11] The projectivist insists that *of course* we take the world and things in it to be the objects of our moral attitudes and judgments, just as we take natural necessity to be a feature of the world. (Though, the argument goes, we give a projective explanation of causality.) The objects of our attitudes and feelings are the objects of concern rather than just those psychological states themselves. Affect is what underlies and underwrites ethical judgment, but in issuing moral judgments we are judging acts, situations, and people's characteristics; we are not talking about our feelings. Blackburn puts it this way: "From the inside, the objects of our passions are their immediate objects: it is the death, the loved one, the sunset, that matters to us. It is not our own state of satisfaction or pleasure. Must projectivism struggle with this fact, or disown it? Is it that we projectivists, at the crucial moment when we are about to save the child, throw ourselves on the grenade, walk out in the snow, will think, 'Oh, it's only me and my desires or other conative pressures—forget it'?"[12] This is a constructive acknowledgment of the phenomenological facts, but it is not clear that it succeeds in supporting the case for antirealism. There remain questions about how our attitudes, responses, and desires are regulated by the features of the world that is their object. It will not do to just make the antireductionist point that the matter is internal to moralizing. It *is* internal to it, but what we are interested in is an explication of the normative authority of claims within moralizing.

REASON AND HABITS

This is where we can ask what it is that the realist puts "on top of the story" but is free-riding and doing no explanatory work. One important aspect of the matter is to distinguish what is to count as 'out there' in its own right and what is projected. Consider a non-ethical context. It would be strange to hold that there are creatures that are just animals, while their being mammals or their being carnivores is to be explained projectively or in terms of conceptual schemes interpreted antirealistically. What is it that the projectivist is going to settle on as being there independent of projection, and what is going to drive that determination? Is being mammalian projected onto being an animal? Is that a convention of apparently successful projection but not more than that? Or is being an animal projected onto being a physical object? This is how the "only primary qualities are real" view, or the view that only the entities posited by a certain level of scientific theorizing are real does indeed get us into trouble. Or, when we look up in the sky and see a group of geese flying in a certain formation and in a certain direction at a specific time of year, do we project onto those facts that the geese are migrating? Unless there is a special and very powerful reason to countenance as real only what is posited by a certain level of scientific theory, we are not precluded from finding that various kinds of things, accessible to us through concepts at various levels of description, are properly interpreted realistically.

Granted, there are distinctive difficulties having to do with values, and their case is not exactly like the cases of other kinds of properties and entities. In addition, it is clear that there are indeed various kinds of features that plainly are projected, features such as being disgusting or being surprising. In these, as in the cases of color perception, there are certainly causal accounts of why we make the judgments we do. The projections are not haphazard. Still, there is a point in distinguishing the status of an attribution of 'disgusting' from the attribution of 'red.' We can haggle about the precise analysis, but whatever we settle on, it should register that distinction. Certainly the connections with affect and the action-guiding dimension of ethical considerations involve their own concerns. Still, it is not at all clear just how the projectivist is to determine what counts as projected, and what is being perceived or detected but not projected (on any plausible, adequately rich construal of perception and detection). This is not a license to posit the existence of values, but it points in the direction that ethical features are no worse off than many kinds of non-ethical features that are correctly interpreted realistically. We will see in particular that the fact that there is a role for receptivity and sensibility in ethical judgment does not diminish the realism of what is judged.

In following a Humean strategy we would interpret a certain family of practices, say, the practices of causal reasoning, or the practices of moral judgment, as being grounded in certain habits of mind, and these habits are not in their own right cognitive habits. Blackburn says that projectivism in ethics has in its favor "the possibility of identifying the [moral] commitment in a way that contrasts it usefully with belief, and a 'neat, natural account' of why the state that it is should exist."[13] There is a rational structure to the ethical practices based upon commitments, but the habits themselves do not register or represent facts or properties in the world. The rationality is in the *superstructure* of judgments, not in what *grounds* them. There can be rationality in the use of concepts and in the consistent universalization of judgments without the basis for the concepts and the judgments being itself cognitive. This, I suggest, is prescriptivity or conative force, without rational authority, and it is a weakness in the projectivist account.

The projectivist will deny that there is a role for reason in determining normative matters and in motivating action, except in what are ultimately instrumental and systematizing respects. I say 'ultimately' because reason has a richer role than just matching means to ends. A projectivist account can make room for consideration of passions and desires across a number of dimensions, in light of various concerns. Hume himself emphasized the role of factual understanding and reasoning in making moral judgments and in moral disputes. The ontological resources may be austere, but the view is not simplistic. Still, in the end, moral judgment is attitudinizing at the bottom, even if at various levels there is a role for reason. There are cognitive issues involved in ascertaining the coherence and consistency with which one uses ethical concepts, but the concepts themselves are not concepts of value understood in a manner that is appropriately interpreted as cognitive. The issue of what has intrinsic ethical value is not itself a matter for cognition. Ultimately, value is a matter of propensity and sentiment, coordinated with a factual understanding of how best to realize what we care about.

On the resources projectivism is limited to, it is possible that cruel actions are not *wrong*. A projective interpretation of value-supervenience permits that result because the fact that we find value supervening where it does is, in an important sense, accidental. The values could have settled elsewhere. It is true that if we were quite different sorts of creatures, with different susceptibilities and modes of affect, then different things would matter to us, or things would matter to us in different ways. That is not the point directly at issue. Rather, the objection to projectivism concerns what resources there are for assessing ethical judgments and sorting the sound ones from the unsound ones. Though projectivism requires consistency in judgment, it is permissive with respect to normative content, and that is the sense in which the location of supervenience is accidental. Perhaps we get our judgments right. Still, the norms of judgment are not cognitively guided and informed. Our metaethic should not allow for the possibility that cruelty is not wrong.

The response might be, "Well, our values haven't settled just anywhere, have they? We can point to the relevant natural facts that are the grounds for these judgments. So, we are quite clear about what makes cruelty wrong."[14] After all, the judgments are judgments for us, not for intellectual beings without bodies, and not for beings with affective natures utterly unlike ours. If we are then told "Anyone who is not morally incompetent can point to the relevant kinds of factual considerations. And anyone who does not respond to cruelty as wrong has disordered moral sensibility," we can agree. The crucial point, however, is that the norms that regulate the responses are not simply more expressions of attitude. Either the norms are regulated by cognitive considerations, or it is difficult to see why they should have any authority as norms except by virtue of the weight of consensus, which may or may not be arrived at rationally, or by virtue of the energy of affect or firmness of attitude. Hume himself took consensus very seriously and the alignment of agents' judgments with those of others was an important part of his account. Moral judgments, in his view, needed public validation. Are there, though, the materials, with the right properties, to make that consensus more than contingent congruence of affect? Is validation more than consensual ratification?

If attitude and sensibility are determinative with respect to valuative judgment, then it is very difficult to see how it is that actual responses do not, in fact, have a decisive role with respect to values. The projectivist will remind us that the facts and properties of things that provide the grounds for the judgment that cruelty is wrong. It is not simply a matter of how we happen to feel in the instance. The concern is that in these antirealist terms ethical norms are decomposable into the natural fact that there are certain non-rational habits or attitudes and certain patterns of relation between those non-rational habits or attitudes and facts and features of situations. The combination of the normativity of concept-use, conative energy and affect supply all of the normativity that ethics requires (so the argument goes). But, again, if values supervene projectively, they have the metaphysical freedom to be at home anywhere, even if they have to meet a requirement of consistency. Within the formal boundaries set by that, they can alight on anything.

Consequently, we can say that projective supervenience could be *ballistic*. It could be unregulated in its "gilding or staining" natural properties, as long as it has a formally rational structure. The way in which projective supervenience can be ballistic can be seen by examining the relation between the 'inside' and the 'outside.' Blackburn says "Now it is not possible to hold an attitude to a thing because of its possessing certain properties and, at the same time, not hold that attitude to another thing that is believed to have the same properties."[15] Projective supervenience needs to meet that condition, but how it does so leaves it unclear what considerations explain how something more or something other than our actual responses is determinative of values. The person who gets things 'wrong' prescribes or projects differently, but what then is the ground for deciding what is wrong with that apart from it being different? Consistency is one thing, and a very important one, but there are many ways of being consistent.

What is needed in order to explain the cognitivist form and truth-evaluability of ethical thought and discourse is an interpretation of the relevant habits of judgment that shows how they are rational with respect to comprehension, not only with respect to the formal features of reasoning. What is needed is an interpretation in which an agent who is fluent in the use of ethical concepts has developed habits of comprehension of certain kinds of ethical significance. The habit is a mode of understanding, of recognizing moral features, not just an affective or conative disposition employed in policies of reasoning.

In explicating Aristotelian moral realism, Stephen Everson claims that the defender of realism "has a ready explanation for the acquisition of evaluative concepts, of course. He can say that what one acquires in acquiring such a concept is precisely a sensitivity to the way things are. What secures the relevant conceptual ability is that one comes to spot that the set of things in question are relevantly similar—and will claim that the relevant similarity can only be captured by using the concept itself. The best explanation, he will claim, both of suitable subjects' convergence in evaluative beliefs and of their ability to become suitable by acquiring the relevant concepts will require that things are, generally speaking, as they are believed to be."[16] What separates the realist and antirealist positions is the contrast between their views of the cognitive content of the concepts deployed in moral thought. Unless the correct use of ethical concepts registers a cognitive appreciation of what the facts ethically count for, or, if you like, what are the moral facts, there will not be the regulation by factual considerations that will enable us to articulate the boundaries of acceptable ethical norms, nor to determine the responses we should have. This is to say that sensibility or attitude is not the sole, ultimate touchstone of normativity. The objectivity of norms for the use of ethical concepts has a cognitivist dimension that the architecture of projectivism tries to preserve but which its materials cannot supply. Projectivism can supply norms. What it cannot supply is a reason to endorse those norms, other than the fact that those who do endorse them are, in doing so, willing to regard them as correct. Many different sets of norms, each endorsed in a stable manner, could be taken to fix ethical systems, meeting requirements of consistency and making appeals to facts to settle disputes and so forth. Their efficacy as ethical norms would not be in doubt as long as there is stability of endorsement. Nor would there be any reason for those who endorsed the norms to consider taking a critical stance toward them, or to exhibiting a willingness to more fully consider whether their judgments are adequately and accurately responsive to moral reality. In any event, even if they did act on such concern, taking a more critical stance would essentially be more attitudinizing.

Nor will a background of considerations about say, evolutionary fitness, make up the deficit. A naturalistic account of the presence or adaptive advantage of conative states and reactive attitudes does indeed help account for the ethical significance of certain issues. That we are here at all with the sensibility and susceptibility that make possible the full range of human virtue and vice is a tale of adaptive advantage. This we can grant without any threat to ethical realism. What the evolutionary account cannot do is settle the issue of which concepts are to be deployed in ethical judgment and in just what ways.

More than a century ago T. H. Huxley wrote, "I have termed this evolution of the feelings out of which the primitive bonds of human society are so largely forged, into the organized and personified sympathy we call conscience, the ethical process."[17] The ethical process, which is itself made possible by the process of natural selection by which the human species came to be, is, he thinks, in conflict with what he called the "cosmic process," the constant, lethal struggle for existence. A crucial part of the ethical process is that by which "It becomes impossible to imagine some acts without disapprobation, or others without approbation of the actor, whether he be one's self or any one else. We come to think in the acquired dialect of morals. An artificial personality, the 'man within,' as Adam Smith calls conscience, is built up beside the natural personality. He is the watch-man of society, charged to restrain the anti-social tendencies of the natural man within the limits required by social welfare."[18]

Huxley argued that of course the capacities we have for both virtue and vice are products of the process of evolution by natural selection. Reading just the quoted passages gives the impression that he is basically putting a Humean theory of moral sentiments on an evolutionary basis. Huxley's view, however, included another insight. He noted that "as the immoral sentiments have no less been evolved, there is, so far, as much natural sanction for the one as the other. The thief and the murderer follow nature just as much as the philanthropist. Cosmic evolution may teach us how the good and the evil tendencies of man may have come about; but, in itself, it is incompetent to furnish any better reason why what we call good is preferable to what we call evil than we had before."[19] We do indeed have good instrumental reasons to approve of and encourage moral habits rather than immoral habits. They enable us to cooperate, they reduce insecurity, they promote trust and mutual concern and assistance, and so forth. The more we encourage the "ethical process" the less likely we are to make true the "gladiatorial theory of existence"[20] that some Social Darwinists claimed to read off of the natural facts. However, with respect to what should be the norms of the moral world, the theory of selective advantage is incomplete at the crucial point, the point where we need to consider what those features of sensibility and those motivational tendencies should count for in rationally warranted actions and responses.

The adaptive merits of a complex repertoire of behaviors do not, on their own, constitute ethical merits even if there is substantial overlap between what is adaptively selected and what is ethically endorsed. We still need non-instrumental ethical thought to ascertain what the norms should be, given the huge repertoire of capacities and tendencies that the process of natural selection yields. This is why moralizing involves practical *comprehension*, or practical cognition, and not just practical *reasoning*. What is comprehended are realistic ethical considerations.

REASON AND SENSIBILITY

We have seen that the objectivity of ethical considerations leaves open the possibility that they may not be accessible to all rational agents. An agent's ethical comprehension depends upon the agent's character, upon his realized capacities for receptivity and discrimination and the valuative commitments he has already formed. That character may be enabling or it may be disabling. The discriminations and calibrations involved in ethical judgment and reasoning require various types of sensitivity and receptivity that are neither 'merely' affective nor 'purely' intellectual. Ethical value is not an object grasped by intellectual insight though fluency with ethical concepts is cognitive fluency, involving recognition of features that are not projections. The way in which wrongness is a feature of cruelty is quite different from the way in which being relaxing is a feature of a certain kind of sound. Similarly, the cognitive competencies involved in the respective recognitions are different. An agent's sensibility is not only that through which he or she is affected, it is also an ingredient in the agent's modes of perception. Attitude and perspective; reactive dispositions; a sense of what matters and what counts and in what ways—all this is involved in the agent's grasp and appreciation of ethically relevant considerations, though our reactions are not constitutive of ethical properties. The role of sensibility in perception is fairly clear in examples of what we might call 'moral blindness,' when there is no reason to think that the agent is cognitively or rationally defective in a way that exempts him from blame. The habits of mind that figure in making such judgments are not decomposable into factual content *plus* an affective laminate or projection. This is why it is plausible to speak of ethical perception, as long as we are careful not to misrepresent it as being just like perceiving, say, yellow, because in the ethical case what is at issue is the agent's recognition of considerations as reasons.

In "Values and Secondary Qualities," McDowell argues that error-theory and projectivism both misinterpret the status of secondary qualities. There is a perfectly respectable sense in which secondary qualities can be taken to be objective, even though they are not to be assimilated to primary qualities. "A secondary quality is a property the ascription of which to an object is not adequately understood except as true, if it is true, in virtue of the object's disposition to present a certain sort of perceptual appearance: specifically, an appearance characterizable by using a word for the property itself to say how the object perceptually appears."[21] Such qualities cannot be "adequately understood otherwise than in terms of dispositions to give rise to subjective states."[22] But that does not lower their status as features of things in the world. The chief upshot of this, though, is not that there is an analogy between the perception of secondary qualities and the perception of ethical features. It is not the issue of *perception* that is the key matter here. The analogy is between the *objective status* of secondary qualities and the status of ethical features. As far as objectivity is concerned, the former are not subjective or projected in the way that they are often portrayed to be, and the latter are not worse off than the former.

Our options are not limited to antirealism and an ontologically problematic "external reading"[23] in the way Blackburn uses that expression. (His is a pejorative use, implying that there would have to be not only ontological exotica but also equally ineffable epistemological faculties to detect them. This is one of the most oft-repeated criticisms of realism and one that is not merited by what is said by most realists.) As we have seen, the antirealist version of truth-evaluability could be constructed from norms in such a way that while truth is parasitical on the norms, the norms are not truth-evaluable. The antirealist could insist that the norms *are* truth-evaluable, in the sense that "To think that a moral proposition is true is to concur in an attitude to its subject".[24] The difficulty in this has already been identified; namely, facts about attitude can explicate conative force but not normative authority. Projectivism inadequately explicates the difference between being satisfied with practices of judgment on the one hand, and, on the other, being attuned to and correctly appreciating ethical considerations. Antirealism domesticates the criteria of truth-evaluability to non-rational habits of mind. The naturalistic explanation of the presence of these habits will account for all of them, whatever they are, giving none of them an ethically privileged status. In doing so, it renders mysterious the issue of why some deployments of concepts reflect correct normative understanding and others do not, except by contingent consensus. We can, of course, say that some statements and claims are true and others are not, but this is hollow truth not plain truth. We might arrive at these conclusions on the basis of argument and reflection. There is no impediment to full dress rational consideration of our ethical judgments. But it is a performance in the costume of cognitivism, and basic valuative commitments will remain non-rational, attitudinal. The problem with the view is not that it assigns a crucial role to sensibility but that it misinterprets what can make sensibility ethical sensibility, the kind that is ingredient in ethical discourse and practice amenable to being rationally informed, adjusted, articulated, and elaborated. Projectivism cannot deliver the moralizing it claims to, because in order to do so it must make use of the realist resources it officially repudiates.

Ethical realism is subject-involving realism. Values are not ontological exotica that are just brutely there. Ethical value is value for human beings, but that does not deflate its realism. To echo Blackburn's remark about respecting the wrong things, realism seems committed to exotica only if we think Platonic value is the only kind realist value could be. But we need not think that. Ethical realism is realism because ethical judgments and claims are grounded in reasons and understanding sufficient for truth-evaluability that is not wholly domesticated to norms of assertibility. We can say that there are moral facts in the sense that there are true moral judgments and that the concepts involved in making the judgments are to be interpreted realistically. There is nothing mysterious about ethical realism unless one thinks it is a mystery that one must be cognitively and affectively well ordered in order to make sound sense of ethical considerations and in order to be able to recognize the truth or falsity of ethical claims. The projectivist might say that he can accept all of that but does not see why it counts as realism. The difference is in what is built into being cognitively well ordered. For the projectivist, being cognitively well ordered is not a matter of employing realistically interpreted concepts. Projectivist cognitivism is formal, not contentful.

The metaethical debate is relevant to issues in moral psychology. The weak agent, in contrast to the disabled agent, has a correct understanding of what is required but fails to enact that understanding. His perception of a situation is 'mixed,' made ambivalent by affect (desire, passion, reactive emotion). In judging or in acting (or in both) his habits are rationally imperfect on account of susceptibility to distraction. His regret is not over not having known what he knows now but over having known it and having succumbed to distraction. The vicious agent and the ethically disabled one do not possess those imperfect habits of perception and reasoning. They have bad cognitive habits and do not see situations in the ways that make the weak agent ambivalent. And as we have seen, this corruption or ignorance is often not responsibility-defeating.

The ethically disabled agent is deploying concepts in ways that are disfigured, and he may have false beliefs (as in various kinds of bigotry, for example). The result is that his deliberation may be careful and detailed but guided by the wrong sorts of concerns. "Should we just kill this guy or wait and see if he can do this next job and do it right?" wonders the crime boss. "Should we use the available rolling stock to transport new inmates to the camps, or should we use it to move the present ones away from the path of the advancing enemy?" These are deliberative projects in which practical reason, norms, and values, no matter how perverse, may be fully involved. Or we can imagine an amoral subordinate, who without any reflective or critical reaction takes instructions from the murderous crime boss or the political leader who is directing a policy of mass killing. He, too, may be an example of ethical disability. He has no distinctive commitment to the ends he is knowingly serving, but neither does he make any ethical objection to them, perhaps not even to himself. He does not endorse, and he does not criticize.

The difference between the ethically capable and the ethically disabled is not that the former act on principles and the latter act on passions or desires. It is a difference concerning what is recognized as a requirement given one's comprehension of the world. The ethically disabled agent may use concepts with a high level of specious fluency. The ethically capable agent's fluency is not specious, though it may be incomplete, a bit clumsy, and deployed in an irresolute manner. The disabled agent lacks comprehension, and, given the collaboration of his sensibility and his understanding, he may be nearly unreachable with respect to improving his appreciation of ethical matters.

THE PARTICULARISM OF REALISM

Earlier we noted realism's shift away from super-general concepts such as 'good' and 'right.' In making careful, fact-sensitive ethical judgments we do not apply a grid of principles to the world.[25] Rather, we aim at a fuller appreciation of the details and complexity of this or that particular concrete way the world is in order to ascertain what to do. Platts has made the point as follows. "Moral concepts have a kind of semantic depth. Starting from our austere grasp upon these concepts, together perhaps with some practical grasp upon the conditions of their application, we can proceed to investigate, to experience, the features of the real world answering to these concepts. Precisely because of the realistic account given of these concepts and of our grasp upon them—precisely because they are designed to pick out features of the world of indefinite complexity in ways that transcend our practical understanding—this process of investigation through experience can, and should, proceed without end."[26]

Moral concepts are indefinable in some of the same ways that natural kind concepts are. There is often no fixed, closed set of terms that specifies an equivalent for them. More and more is found out about what it is to be a thing of some specific kind, and there is no clean break between what is 'built into' the meaning and what else is true of things of that kind. In both cases, our fluency with the relevant concepts increases as we learn more about what they refer to, and we come to realize that the contents of our conceptions can be indefinitely enlarged.

Consider the use of concepts by a child. A seven-year-old is likely to use the concepts *dog* and *fair* in ways that are closely regulated by his own experience with their referents, and it is likely that his use of those concepts is not very discriminating. There are many distinctions among dogs and among things that are fair of which he is, as yet, unaware. With enlarged experience there will be added complexity in his conceptions and the increasing ability to make many relevant distinctions. His initial understandings of what is a dog and what is fair will then seem like blunt instruments, which can do a certain job (they reliably tether him to real referents), but there are many more skilled jobs to do with those concepts. He also learns about the connections between his understanding of those things and many other things. In the case of *dog*, there will be connections with *mammal, domestication, carnivorous*, and so on. In the case of *fair* there will be connections with *impartiality, unselfish*, what is *owed*, one's *share*, and so forth. In neither case are these connections fully specifiable as analytic truths. They depend on the extent of a comprehension that must be empirically informed.

In an agent's developing competence with ethical concepts (or uses of concepts in ethical contexts) encounter with cases is crucial. Real fluency is not a matter of employing concepts such as 'good' or 'right' in approved ways; it is matter of employing much more specific concepts to the particular features of situations. The explanations of why various cases are instances of this or that specific type of wrongfulness (e.g., treachery, spite, ingratitude) point to a realist interpretation.[27] The explanations are not merely generic (in terms of approval and aversion, for example) and, to the extent that they are adequate, they pick out the specific features that place the phenomena under *those* specific concepts rather than others. The complexity of our array of ethical concepts is underwitten by the realism of the phenomena the concepts refer to in that we are responsive to a large variety of features which figure as different considerations and which merit discrimination in ethical judgment and reasoning. That is to say that realism supplies a better account of how it is that we acquire such a complex repertoire of ethical concepts. Each answers to features that we encounter in experience.

In the judgment of particular cases we can both employ and enlarge our comprehension, not necessarily by finding that a rule or principle applies more widely than we previously thought but by articulating more of the content of the concepts in order to grasp the features of the case. There is scope for more and more specification and increasingly fine discriminations. Of course consistency matters, and there are valid generalizations about the relations between ethically salient features of situations and other features of them. But that is not because (or evidence for the claim that) there are ethical principles that can be deployed in formally structured ethical theory. We may not be able to itemize in a stable, comprehensive manner just what considerations have ethical significance and how much weight they have or be able to determine the relative weights of ethical considerations in complex situations. This inability does not mean that there is nothing to say, that judgment is a matter of inarticulate intuition. There is a difference between fluency with the relevant concepts (which, of course, is required) and there being a system of generalizations and rules that is determinative of judgment. As Platts remarks of ordinary moral life, the problem is not that of squaring our "present judgments with our previous judgments, but that of attending to the full, unobvious moral complexity of the present case. In ordinary moral life, determining our moral judgment about a particular case by means of some rule seizing upon non-moral aspects of that case will simply mean that we neglect the full complexity of that particular case."[28]

Moreover, it is rare that ethical comprehension should be increased by telling or teaching someone general ethical principles. Doing so may help express and clarify an increasing comprehension, but the latter is not itself mainly a matter of grasping principles. Or, it may be a way of drawing attention to certain overlooked features, but it is attention to the features that make for comprehension of cases. The actual process tends to be more a matter of the agent beginning to be responsive to certain considerations and more fully appreciating their weight. Then, as a result of reflection, there is an increasingly articulate, generalizable understanding of the import of those sorts of considerations.

Imagine someone who regularly criticizes or demeans people and who tries to get control or establish 'dominance' in conversational and social situations by exploiting other people's vulnerabilities and making them feel threatened or insecure. It is unlikely that trying to draw this person's attention to a rule of respect or to rights claims or any similarly general notion will bring about the relevant change in his disposition and practice. The agent may realize that his friendships are few or are not fulfilling, and it may occur to him that this has something to do with his own character and behavior. As a result of changing his behavior and trying to establish different habits he may very well come to learn something about the meaning of respect and friendship. The diagnosis of his new understanding or the moral point of it will include showing how instances fall under general concepts or rules, but his understanding of the applicability of those concepts and rules depends upon appreciation of particular situations.

It might be objected that this is to confuse or conflate moral theory with moral psychology, that we have confused how something is brought into view with what is brought into view. It is surely true that rules and criteria have an important role, but it is also true that they are only determinative of judgment in the sense that the relevant concepts are deployed in a manner calibrated to the specific features of the case. What courage requires, what fairness requires, what generosity requires always depends upon the more or less complex character of a situation and its ethically relevant relations to other facts, acts, and situations. The rules apply, but there is a not a system that determines how they apply. That we can give reasons for our judgments and our actions and that those reasons have general significance is not the same as to say that there is a system that specifies the weights and relations of those reasons.

In remarks on whether and how an ethics of virtue is uncodifiable, Gary Watson notes that "this thesis is difficult to evaluate because codifiability seems to be a matter of degree. On the one hand, there are true moral generalizations about conduct, as even the proponents of uncodifiability should agree; on the other hand, the most rigid codifiers should concede that judgment is necessary for interpreting and applying any rules and principles."[29] It would be most implausible to deny that there are significant moral generalizations. In addition, we can certainly identify certain key virtues, and there are important generalizations about what they require, and it is true, of course, that in ethical habituation we typically learn rules first as way of developing the abilities to make judgments. This is a way of drawing the agent's attention and of encouraging competence with certain concepts new to him. He can then use them in more fine-grained and textured ways. Exercising sound judgment is not primarily (and certainly not exclusively) a matter of applying rules and principles. Again, there is an analogy to concepts of natural kinds; our concept of what it is to be a mammal is formulated on the basis of an understanding of members of this and that particular species. It does not have 'stand alone' status, though it can be employed in highly general explanations. We can make important claims about what it is to be a mammal, but they are abstractive generalizations from facts about different specific kinds of creatures we have reason to classify as mammals. What it is to be a mammal depends on what certain animals are like.

It can appear that some ethical principles are a priori if certain ethical considerations have very general applicability and there is a high level of convergence in understanding. We might then think; "Of course this is what is ethically required. Anyone who has not lost their reason or who has thought clearly can see the truth of this principle." We might say this concerning some highly general matter of fairness, for example, or the wrongness of cruelty. Nevertheless, the conviction that some principle is true is not achieved just by reflection on the concepts in it and their relations. Similarly, understanding the connections *between*, say, fairness and courage, or generosity, temperance, and fairness, is not simply a matter of examining concepts. It is a result achieved by experience-informed consideration, in conjunction with the well-ordered dispositions that enable the agent to make the proper acknowledgments.

Consider fairness. What it requires is not susceptible to formulation in a fixed body of rules or principles. Following the rule that one should be fair is analogous in some respects to a kindergarten teacher following the rule "prepare the children for first grade." Doing so involves paying different kinds of attention to each child and interacting with each one in ways calibrated to prepare that child. It involves using the various kinds of available resources in suitably calibrated ways. The overall effort makes demands of various kinds and calls for judgment across a number of dimensions. The rule will not by itself be an adequate guide to the teacher. We might say that fairness always requires treating people in a manner that respects their claims in proper proportion.[30] But then the real work is done in the specification of the relevant claims and their ethical weight. In using concepts competently and with attention to detail the agent's actions will conform to certain rules, for example, being honest, being fair, doing no avoidable harm, and so forth, but his actions will conform by addressing the specific features of particular situations, rather than by an application of general rules.

There is no special reason to think that exhibiting the form of a systematic theory is something that sound ethical thought and reasoning must do. For example, each of us has various ethical obligations to family members, to friends, to people generally. These obligations are diverse in content, weight and in their grounds, and there is no special reason to think that each is a variant, suitably adjusted to circumstances, of a more fundamental principle of obligation. Sometimes an obligation or a requirement is grounded in the position we occupy, or it is grounded in our love for someone, or in the fact that we are indebted to another, or in the fact that we gave our word, and so forth. We can know what many of these responsibilities are, and we can recognize breaches of them without these determinations depending upon a single, fundamental principle or set of principles.

Naturally, the attempt at system can bring to light relations, conflicts, ordering, and so forth. I am not suggesting that it be dispensed with. But neither are there grounds for thinking that system has priority over particular judgments. Explicating particular judgments by embedding them in a wider system can be illuminating without reflecting a necessary feature of their justification. Correspondingly, the virtuous agent acts not primarily because giving assistance or being honest or fulfilling her responsibilities is *right*, but because another needed help, because the agent's opinion was sought, because she has a role to play or an office to perform, and so forth. To do all these things *is* right. The virtuous agent, though, is attending mainly to what is to be done, and not mainly to whether to do the *right* thing.

Whatever general ethical knowledge the agent has, the judgment in the case depends upon ascertaining what is ethically salient in it. Describing some contemporary particularist views, Nancy Sherman writes: "Moral principles still have a use in the moral life, but their use is pedagogic, as when a principle of fidelity is used in reference to particular paradigms, such as intentional lies. Moral justification itself is not ruled out, but it is not to be viewed as subsumptive."[31] There is plenty to say of each case but not in a way that the case is exhibited as an instance of law-like generalizations that are determinative of its ethical content. The identification of what is ethically significant and the determination of what to do depend more directly and more fully on discriminations and employment of conceptual articulateness than on application of rules. Consider the following analogy: There are many different types of bread, with differences in ingredients, in how they are baked, and in their shapes. There are yeast breads and no-rise breads; there are sweet breads and sourdough breads; there are light breads and breads that are heavy, and so on, in remarkable variety. If you are interested in what you are eating, or if you want to understand this part of the food world, your interest is in "what kind of bread is this?" or in "how is this made?" rather than in the question, "what makes something bread?"

Critics of realism often make it sound as though a commitment to moral properties is analogous to some kind of ontological bird-watching: "look, over there; if I am not mistaken, that is a categorical imperative." It is a misrepresentation of realism to characterize it as requiring ineffable value-entities and non-natural faculties to detect those entities. Competence with the relevant concepts is needed in order to comprehend how facts count as ethical considerations, but that is not a special or exotic kind of cognitive ability, nor does it give access to special or exotic features of reality.

I noted at the beginning of this chapter that the central moral psychological claims of this account do not require a realist metaethic. Still, there are reasons in favor of realism, and those claims and a realist metaethic are mutually reinforcing. We are better able to understand why the fact that ethical considerations are objective is not, as such, also a reason for thinking that any rational agent can grasp and appreciate ethical considerations or that an understanding of them will be motivationally effective. We are better able to fathom how agents can be rational and can engage in practical reasoning but in ways that exhibit seriously defective practical comprehension. That there are such agents does seem to be a fact on the ethical landscape, and realism gives the best diagnosis of its existence as well as the best exploration of its perplexity.

Conclusion

We have presented claims about the extent to which character is voluntary, the role of character and sensibility in ethical judgment, the fixity or near-fixity of mature character, claims about conscience, and claims in defense of realism. These are parts of a conception of moral psychology and metaethics largely developed out of resources in Aristotle's philosophy but not intended as an account of Aristotle's ethical philosophy. Virtue-centered realism has considerable merits but some of those merits do not encourage optimism about the ethical capacities of agents. In particular, claims about the effective capacity of agents to ethically self-correct are often exaggerated. One of the merits of the view is that it helps explicate why the objectivity of ethical considerations does not guarantee their accessibility. Another is that it helps explicate the rationale for criticism of agents, for blaming and punishing them, even when they are unresponsive in ethically constructive ways.

The claims about voluntariness and responsibility for one's own character have a central place in the account. Recent discussions of moral luck remind us how easy it is to exaggerate claims for both autonomy and responsibility. When we consider how numerous and how strong are the factors influencing or impinging on who we are and what we do, it can seem that there is virtually no scope left for character to be voluntary.[1] How then *can* it be that persons are responsible for their characters? Chapter 1 explained that the view is not that we each create our own characters or even that we fully intend or foresee the characteristics that become established. We often do not recognize what difference will be made to our states by the actions we perform. It can be said that we sometimes voluntarily bring about dispositions that we did not intend to bring

118

about. It is not necessary that an agent anticipate how a pattern of voluntary activity will affect his own character for the resulting state of character to be voluntary. Sometimes we do anticipate the result or at least try to; often we do neither of those things. Still, the ways in which human beings act and the ways in which they respond are, in significant respects, reflective of commitments, concerns, and judgments that constitute action-guiding conceptions for which they are responsible. As a result, agents are responsible in a substantial respect for the second natures they acquire.

Part of the explanation for this responsibility is that many of the influences on an agent do not do their work independently of the 'uptake' on the part of the agent. Everybody has a story, and temperament and circumstances are important non-voluntary elements of one's story. Still, the sort of person one is, the sorts of persisting, guiding dispositions that shape strategies and policies of action and response are shaped by conceptions of value that are not simply given, determined, or imposed. The ways in which constitutive and circumstantial luck influence an agent depend upon voluntariness though obviously the entry and ongoing presence of these factors in a person's life do not. (Though we can position ourselves to make it more likely that we should have some kinds of luck rather than others. We can exercise a measure of control over who we are among and in what kinds of circumstances we find ourselves.)

Many agents give little thought to the values transmitted to them and to the ethical quality of their dispositions. Those agents still have a substantial measure of responsibility for their characters and their values because of the ways in which their own voluntariness (even if unthoughtfully exercised) is involved in their becoming who they are. There can be responsibility even where the agent does not *take* responsibility. Through voluntary activity we may acquire dispositions that are firmly established but which we wish to alter. Perhaps those dispositions have put us in a place it is very difficult to get away from. There was still voluntariness in the development of the predicament even as we acknowledge the limitations of our ability to now change it in fundamental ways. These limitations may be welcome and admirable if they are limitations on us that are shaped by our virtues. They may also be unwelcome and even ethically disabling.

Several strands of the modern and contemporary discussion of freedom of the will and personhood focus on identification and reflective endorsement of desires and values. For example, Christine Korsgaard argues that: "Reflection gives us a kind of distance from our impulses which both forces us, and enables us, to make laws for ourselves, and it makes those laws normative. To make a law for yourself, however, is at the same time to give expression to a practical conception of your identity. Practical conceptions of our identity determine which of our impulses we will count as reasons."[2] And: "What is not contingent is that you must be governed by *some* conception of your practical identity. For unless you are committed to some conception of your practical identity, you will lose your grip on yourself as having any reason to do one thing rather than another—and with it, your grip on yourself as having any reason to live and act at all."[3]

This can be read in a way that is not at odds with the conception defended here, as long as notions such as "treating one's humanity" do not have too much rationalistic self-consciousness built into them. It can also be read in a more purely Kantian way, putting it in contrast with the present conception of agents. The Kantian reading would put more emphasis on the kinds of ambitious first-person reflective undertakings (in particular, reflective *endorsements*) that Korsgaard describes. In fact, a great deal of voluntary human action is voluntary without reflective regard for what makes it voluntary, without discursive reflective endorsement.

For instance, if I am someone to whom it is very important to be the center of attention, I will act for reasons having to do with trying to be the center of attention. These activities are voluntary and are expressions of my character, even if the reasons for which I act are not reasons I reflectively endorse or to which I give much consideration at all. Still, my acting in those ways expresses my practical, normative identity, and it is activity for which I am responsible. In this respect the voluntariness of the activity contrasts with activity motivated by an unconscious drive, for example, or a condition that would move me to act in specific ways even if I made every effort not to do so. It need not be the enactment of an identification that I settle on after a critical assessment of my desires. I may be that sort of person because I have *not* undertaken that sort of assessment. That inattention, or, if you will, that sort of neglect of the ethical features of our dispositions, is not inattention or neglect that makes the states and the actions they give rise to less than voluntary. This is true of characteristics such as being submissive to authority, or resenting authority, aiming to ingratiate oneself, or being a person of one's word, among others, on a very long list. In exhibiting these characteristics we are typically acting voluntarily, and the entrenchment of these dispositions occurs largely through voluntary action. We have many policies and strategies of action and reaction for which we are responsible but not by virtue of having legislated them, except in the thin sense of ratifying them by enactment. We do not determine practical identities for ourselves by each reasoning our way into one. Instead, as a result of habituation, circumstance, and natural temperament we accept certain sorts of desires and considerations as reasons, certain sorts of passions as apt, and we are able to deploy reason in order to work with those character contents with a view to acceptance, adjustment, or rejection.

The strong Kantian reading of Korsgaard's view is vulnerable in a way analogous to the vulnerability of the Socratic view that virtue is knowledge, though each view does indeed capture something crucial. The Kantian view captures the fact that self-determination and morally sound action depend upon reason. The Socratic view captures the fact that self-determination and morally sound action depend upon a cognitive engagement with reality. In each case the view is overstated in such a way that for action that does not meet a standard of autonomous rationality, or action that is not done in the light of full knowledge, it is problematic that it should be taken to fully be the agent's action. The most plausible view gives proper place to reason and knowledge in action and ethics without narrowly construing agency and ethical action in terms of ideals of rationality and knowledge. An agent's rationality can be invested in action to an extent that makes it voluntary even if it is a disordered exercise of reason or if it reflects defects of knowledge. There are defects of practical reason that are not such as to disqualify the agent as a full-fledged participant in the ethical order, acting in ways that merit attributions of responsibility.

RECAPITULATION

Showing that a human agent's responsibility is not undone by the fact that history, society, and nature have played substantial roles in molding his character was the main task of chapter 1. Those are not forces that come together at a point of action, each with its own determinate magnitude. They are the dimensions across which human action needs to be understood in order not to privilege or discount one or another of its explanatory ingredients. Voluntariness is wider than it is often taken to be, but the ability to change is less robust than it is often taken to be. Reason has a central role in the acquisition of a second nature for which an agent is responsible but not always (or often) by guiding that process through a critical and reflective process of deliberately undertaking to acquire the characteristics that constitute that second nature.

Chapter 2 presented the view that agents can become ethically disabled and remain responsible agents even though they do not or even cannot credit the grounds on which they are judged to act wrongly. Moreover, even where ethical disability reflects the prevailing morality it may still be appropriate to ascribe a full measure of responsibility to people. Their voluntariness and the involvement of their practical reason in what they do and what they value is not automatically lesser on account of large-

scale social or institutional impediments to virtue. The point is not punitive; of course we should acknowledge why people are blind to certain
kinds of moral considerations and why it is improbable that they should
be able to bring them into view. Rather, the point was to give proper
weight to the fact that if we insist that an effective, realized capacity to
know the good and to do it is a condition of moral responsibility then we
will, by that insistence, diminish the responsibility of (large numbers of)
agents who know what they are doing, do it voluntarily, think it is good to
do, and do vicious things.

It is true that ethically disabled agents are less reachable by blame. They
are not likely to respond to it with recognition of their wrong and with
efforts of self-correction. This raises serious perplexities about how blame
is to be addressed to them and about the point of it. (Our main concern
was when we are thinking about blaming contemporary wrongdoers, not
agents distant from us in time.) When it seems blame has virtually no
chance of motivating acknowledgment of wrongdoing, repentance, and
reform, this creates considerable perplexity for those who denounce the
wrongdoing. The agent being blamed does not and perhaps cannot
endorse the values that rationalize blame, but may still seem to be a fully
responsible agent. One option would be to hide the cost of this perplexity
by writing off the responsibility of persistently vicious agents. However,
this strategy risks misrepresenting the extent to which those agents are
acting voluntarily and knowingly. They may not know what is good, but
they know what they are doing and they think it is the thing to do.

Chapter 3 discussed the issue of whether agents are typically capable of
substantially revising their second natures. Given our broad interpretation of voluntariness, it might seem that it should range over that issue as
well. Yet we did not take that view. It is not just that character is not simply
changed by *decision*. It is also an issue of whether the relevant sorts of
acknowledgments can be made and whether having made them, agents
can then go on to act in ways that really alter their dispositions. In general, we cannot say with confidence that just *this* sort of change is enough
to mark a change in character or that a change of *that* sort is not enough,
and so forth. Instead, reasons were given for concluding that our expectations for ethically significant change in character should be quite modest. If a change in character involves coming to a substantially different
appreciation of ethical considerations, then such change cannot be generally expected of people. We may be able to expect them to alter their
behavior, in order to avoid criticism or punishment. They often do so and
can do that without it reflecting or contributing to ethically significant
change. Even if we allow that indeed people do sometimes undergo
changes of character in which their voluntariness has played an important

role, we still need to take seriously the notion that there are responsible ethically disabled agents who, because of their disability, cannot bring into view, and are not motivationally able to engage with the sorts of considerations that would guide a change of character in the direction of virtue. Similarly, the soundly virtuous agent may be unable to seriously countenance practices that would corrupt her character in an enduring, significant manner.

The discussion of Maimonides showed that there might be an important connection between views about the accessibility of objective moral considerations and views about the power of the will. This impression is reinforced by consideration of Kant's moral philosophy. Kant and Maimonides had quite different accounts of the objectivity of ethical considerations but they agreed that moral requirements are not inaccessible by virtue of an agent's character, and an agent's will can be effectively engaged to ethical requirements whatever his history of volition. The present view is that the cognitive grasp of moral considerations, and not just motivational engagement with them, may depend much more fully on what sort of character an agent has.

If the link between objectivity and accessibility is character, then not even the combination of objectivity and rationality will ensure accessibility, much less motivational efficacy. This is what is behind the claim that it is not simply true of rational agents that 'ought' implies 'can.' Their valuative attachments and motivational dispositions can disable them for seeing what they ought to do, and disable them for being effectively capable of doing it, or both. There is a thin sense in which we can say of such agents that they "could have known better"; they were not constitutionally incapacitated for having acquired that knowledge. But, given the sorts of agents they actually are, and their willingness to persist in being those ways, it may not be the case that they could, in the instance, know better. The really dreadful person may be beyond our influence and beyond our reach, whether compassionate or punitive, but may still be within the scope of a common moral world with us. The story of his dreadfulness may not exempt him from moral evaluation.

There is no standpoint of character-independent practical rationality from which each agent can be expected to achieve a grasp of ethical requirements. Character has a crucial role in facilitating access to them, and it can be a serious impediment to access. The tendency of characteristics to become fixed can sustain virtue, and it can also put it and the aspiration to it further and further out of reach. Additional arguments in support of this were given in the discussion of conscience in chapter 4. That chapter showed that interpretations of conscience as an innate capacity to grasp true ethical principles or as an innate motivational source for right action are unnecessary and implausible. The work that conscience is often said to do can be explained in terms of features of agents' second natures, in terms of certain acquired habits of attention and moral effort.

In chapter 5 we argued that there is a case for a realist metaethic and tried to show how it explanatorily coheres with the fact that ethical considerations may be inaccessible to some agents. Realism's credentials were reinforced by its fit with the moral psychological claims and by antirealism's difficulty with adequately accounting for normative authority. In addition, the interpretation of realism comports well with the notion that in rational action people aim at what they take to be good without this requiring a commitment to an intrinsic disposition to know or to enact what is in fact good. The extent to which that capacity is developed and exercised depends upon the social world, the individual's 'story,' the agent's voluntariness, and the dispositions of the agent, both natural and acquired.

FINAL OBSERVATIONS

In concluding, I shall a make a few additional remarks about the notion that human beings are naturally disposed to the good. This issue was raised earlier, at the end of the discussion of conscience. However, having offered some defense of virtue-centered realism, it is a particularly apt topic with which to close.

In the ancient and medieval teleological view normativity was built into the world and into human nature. In some of the most influential theories, the virtues were needed for the completion or perfection of one's nature. There was no distinctive issue about whether there were reasons to lead an ethically sound life. Or rather, there was not understood to be a metaphysical or epistemic gap between human nature and ethical value and requirements. Maybe not all agents could see the point of leading virtuous lives, but what they would see, if they could see the point, was that to do so is to actualize just the excellences that are proper to their nature. Not to actualize those excellences would be tantamount to not successfully being a human being in an important sense. The agent's condition would be more (or less, perhaps we should say) than just having vices or ethical defects. The complete reality of a human being was realized by excellences proper to the essence of members of humankind. An excellent example of the view is Aquinas, who is also a good example of the view that human beings have a natural tendency to pursue their good. He writes, "Therefore, since the rational soul is the proper form of man, there is in every man a natural inclination to act according to reason; and this is to act according to virtue."[4]

The idea was not the quite implausible one that people will acquire the virtues unless something deflects them from that course. Rather, it was that there are reasons for an agent to acquire and exercise the virtues simply because of the nature of the agent. There is a mode of perfective activity grounded in a kind-specific essence. Moreover, being good is a good to the agent who is good, and the virtuous agent's interest coincides with what in fact makes for human excellence. The justificatory concerns of modern philosophy, concerns about the relation between nature and norm or fact and value, are not in evidence in this view, in large part on account of confidence in the teleological understanding of the world of which it was part.

Aquinas built an inclination to ethical good into human nature explicitly through his account of *synderesis* and natural law. There is not only an overall good to which human nature is inclined, but the human being also has a grasp of first principles of practical reason to direct him to it. In that respect, Aquinas's view departed somewhat from Aristotle's, which did not make the same provisions for knowledge (even if only highly general knowledge) of human good. According to the present view, there are indeed objective human goods, the virtues are excellences through which an agent can grasp what is good and act from concern for it, and the virtuous agent enjoys doing so. However, this does not involve a commitment to the claim that there is an overall good to which human beings are disposed in the sense that when they pursue what is not good, we should say that they have been somehow turned from their natural disposition.

What we can say is that there is a tendency to enjoy what is good, given the cognitive, affective, and appetitive capacities of the human constitution, and that the best and most enduring goods for a human being can be appreciated as such when they are realized. It might be argued that if the good is naturally pleasing it is so because of a natural inclination towards it. However, a human being can find it 'naturally pleasing' even if there is no effective innate tendency to seek or to do what is really good as a feature of a common human nature. 'Naturally' can mean 'right for' or 'suited to the nature of' without also involving an internal principal of motion or tendency in that direction. The claim that virtuous activity is naturally pleasing can be vindicated by reflection upon ethical practice and phenomenology even if it is not embedded in a metaphysical perfectionism. Perfectionism might be vindicated, but the vindication would take place through reflection on ethics rather than as a result coming from metaphysics to ethics. The most plausible moral anthropology may indeed be perfectionist without it being a special case of a global perfectionism.

In the *Rhetoric*, Aristotle says of pleasure that it is "a movement by which the soul as a whole is consciously brought into its normal state of being" (1369b 34). In his view, pleasure is supervenient upon activity, with better pleasures supervening on better activities. That is the sort of teleology about which there is now a good deal of skepticism, much of it legitimate. It is legitimate if perfectionism is restricted to a single, uniquely best life for a human being and there is no scope for considerations of plurality of values and incommensurability. Its legitimacy weakens when we acknowledge that there are virtuous activities that are naturally pleasing for any ethically sound human being, even if they do not wholly comprise a uniquely best form of life activity. It is good to have the virtues and the virtuous agent is positioned to understand and appreciate (enjoy) their intrinsic value.

This is not to say that the virtuous agent acts well in order to attain the enjoyment that supervenes on doing so. The virtuous agent acts well because it is his second nature to do what is ethically required. This is not a type of stealth-hedonism. There are types of pleasure only accessible to virtuous agents but those agents do not act virtuously so that they may achieve those pleasures. It can both be the case that virtuous activity is necessary for certain distinctive types of pleasure, and that the virtuous agent does what virtue requires because of his concern for good. That acting well is pleasing may reinforce and sustain virtue but the virtuous agent acts well for its own sake, being guided by a right comprehension of good. We can say that the virtuous agent desires to act well, but this is not a desire independent of his comprehension of good. We can also say that the virtuous agent has a general aspiration to act well, and so may the continent agent. In that respect, there is a desire or concern that is not just the same thing as the agent's comprehension of value. But that desire or concern is not an independent state of mind, contingently connected to the agent's beliefs about ethical value. It is not a 'Humean' desire with a stand-alone status.

To be ethically disabled is bad, not just because the vicious agent harms others but because it is a loss to that agent. It is a loss not just because the agent has false beliefs about ethical matters, but also because ethical disability is a way of being alienated from reality and estranged from goods that can be enjoyed without self-deception or ignorance. Granted, the ethically disabled agent does not experience his condition as involving this loss. This agent is not employing the valuations that come with the understanding possessed by the virtuous agent, so he does not miss the pleasures that are available to the virtuous agent. That does not show that human good or ethical reasons are subjective but that the ethically disordered or disabled agent may not experience his state as frustrating, painful, or regrettable. It is symptomatic of the fact that certain habits of judgment and valuation are needed in order to recognize what virtue requires and to find it worthwhile to do what it requires. It is almost certainly a mistake to regard a conception of the virtuous agent as indicating the natural tendencies of human nature just so long as they have not been perverted or disordered.

As we have noted, people are of course sometimes able to make efforts to reorient themselves toward what is good. This must be recognized even though substantial change of mature character is by no means common or easy. There are people who, for example, respond to being forgiven and acknowledge their ethical deficiencies and undertake to do something about them. They sometimes succeed. There are people who reconsider their lives and undertake to make substantial changes for the better in how they lead them. Sometimes they do this late in life but still the change seems to be genuine. The case for ethical disability need not (implausibly) rule this out. It was intended to emphasize the fact that the capacity for such change is not a constantly present feature of our nature as rational agents. Moreover, it is not clear that this is a return to a natural or innate disposition. Rather, there is the capacity to acquire good habits (helped or hindered by luck), and there is often some capacity to restore them when they have become corrupted.

If the sort of broadly Aristotelian naturalism described here is a correct general account of ethics and moral psychology then perhaps we have to reconcile ourselves not only to the reality of vice in rational agents but also to ethical disability and the perplexities it gives rise to. In this important way the view differs from the Kantian and the Jewish and Christian views. The rationality of agents does not ensure that they can effectively ethically self-correct. It would be misleading to say that the ethically disabled agent is just a vicious agent who remains vicious. That would leave it open that to reorient himself toward virtue is still a real, practical possibility for him and that because he ought to do so he can do so. Disability is not just persistence in vice, and the way in which the agent is cut off from good and from excellence may not be reparable. That is the possibility we need to take more seriously and it raises issues in addition to those raised by vice where there is not disability. The enormity of a crime is one thing; whether an agent is ethically reachable is another. In the religious tradition grace underwrites the possibility of ethical perfection. In the Jewish tradition it is through the gift of the Law that the discipline of perfection is known, and volition can always re-engage us to the Law. In the Christian tradition, grace can turn the soul toward perfection, even if it is established in bad habits. The religious tradition acknowledges that we need help, has faith that we get it, and also has faith that it is all the help we need. The resources of naturalism on their own cannot underwrite ethical perfection and redemption to the same extent.

Naturalistic and rationalistic ethics have largely taken over the redemptive optimism of the religious tradition but without adequately acknowledging the difference that is made once theism is dropped out of moral psychology and the metaphysics of morals. The examination of this difference makes it plain that in thinkers such as Maimonides and Aquinas the differences made by theism were not mere accessories to, say, an Aristotelian ethical naturalism. The differences were fundamental and they significantly altered moral psychology and moral epistemology. Indeed, in Maimonides' case it would be fair to say that he used Aristotelian idiom to present a moral psychology that is quite un-Aristotelian, the divergence due in large part to a metaphysics of morals that is centered on elements simply not found in Aristotle's ethical philosophy.

It is necessary to take seriously second nature as a key to moral psychology and to take seriously the role of character in ethical cognition. The practical rationality of human beings is rationality that operates through second nature, and there is no route from rationality to virtue that does not go through second nature. The point is not that we should have a much more modest conception of the virtues or less exalted ideals. It is that we should represent to ourselves more accurately the ways in which vice disfigures our lives and the ways in which it can distort our understanding without also signaling to us that it has done so. Vice is voluntary, and it is rational agents who are vicious. Their cruelty, their dishonesty, their callousness, and the rest are not always lapses from or violations of standards and principles that of course they recognize. Often, they do not recognize correct ethical standards and principles, and, at a certain point, though they are still fully participants in the ethical world, they may not be able to do so.

In ethical life the danger is that ethical disability is often attributed too quickly, too punitively, and without a proper measure of concerned engagement with those so regarded. It is not only that we are too quick to condemn and that we often condemn too harshly for vicious acts but also that we sometimes ethically abandon each other and we are too willing to regard others as incorrigible. In practice, the task is to guard against too quickly making the judgment of disability and claiming to find it where it is not. In moral theorizing, the error has been inattention to it or implausible attempts to explain it away. What is needed is not a contraction of our moral aspirations but an adjustment of our theories to better describe the features of the moral world and orient us to them.

Notes

Introduction

[1] There are agents who have 'unnatural' desires or who are otherwise constitutionally incapacitated for virtue or who are insane. Of course, those agents are less than fully responsible for their characters and actions. They are ethically disabled but not as a result of the exercise of their own voluntariness. The distinction between these types of agents will be discussed in what follows.

[2] I have gotten under way with that project. See my "Luck and Retribution," in *Philosophy* 74 (October 1999): 535–55.

[3] My own view is that the prospects for moral theory as a project of fashioning a system of principles and an ordering of the weights of various kinds of moral considerations are easily exaggerated. If we get the metaethics and the moral psychology right, there does not seem to me to be a major, independent project of moral theory construction in a formal sense. There are indeed important general principles and there are moral requirements that can be specified in quite definite ways. But I do not think that we can locate them in a fixed, comprehensive system of moral principles and requirements. While I defend realism about ethical considerations, I am skeptical of the aspirations of moral theory. Here I merely make the remark and do not argue for the view.

[4] Maimonides holds that ethical requirements are given in revealed Law and it is this, which, in his view, accounts for their accessibility. In Maimonides' view, because ethical considerations are revealed, they are accessible and agents can reasonably be expected to alter their dispositions in the direction of virtue. It is possible for them to know what to do in order to succeed at that, and they have the volitional capacity to do so, no matter how long-established their states of character. Later, especially in chapter 3, I will say more about the contrast between the theistic and non-theistic views and the connections between moral psychology and the accessibility of ethical requirements.

1. Voluntariness and Habits

[1] Some of the arguments in this chapter are developments of arguments in my article, "The Virtues of Externalism," *Southern Journal of Philosophy* 34 (1996): 285–99.

[2] Ledger Wood, for example, says that "The arguments of the free-willist are for the most part humanistic and non-scientific in character" (p. 388) and later in the same article, says that while "the evidence for the free will doctrine is largely humanistic and moralistic, the case for determinism is an appeal to scientific evidence" (p. 395). It is clear what he reads into this difference. *Philosophy* 16 (1941): 386–99.

[3] Gregory Trianosky, "Natural Affection and Responsibility for Character," in *Identity, Character, and Morality,* ed. Owen Flanagan and Amélie Oksenberg Rorty (Cambridge: MIT Press, 1990), p. 106.

[4] There is juvenile practical reasoning which is sufficient for attributions of responsibility even in quite young children. For example, if a five year old is running back and forth across the room until it becomes very annoying, a reprimand may bring it to a stop. The running was voluntary but perhaps not an activity resulting from deliberation. When the child starts in again, in order to test the patience of the adults, that may very well be deliberate. There are deliberate actions in a much deeper sense, in that they are parts of the overall project of leading a certain kind of life. But even in the illustration above, the individual's capacities for practical reason are at work and the idiom of responsibility fits the case.

[5] A defender of hard determinism might argue that talk of voluntariness, agency, and moral responsibility is just a misleading way of saying that among the causes of some actions are certain kinds of internal states of the individual. On this line of argument, even when we do what we want, in the light of foreseen consequences, and on the basis of deliberation, that is no less the result of causes than when I fall into the water because someone sneaks up behind me and pushes me off the diving board. There is only a difference in the kinds of causes. (This, in fact, is often part of the libertarian incompatibilist's objection to compatibilism; viz., causation is causation.) There clearly is a difference, relevant to ascribing responsibility, between jumping off the diving board in order to show off for a particular pool-side observer, and being shoved off of it. The difference is more vivid if, for example, I land on someone in the water and injure that person. If I was jumping in order to show off, I am culpably negligent for not being more careful. If I was shoved, the situation and the appropriate attitude to the event of injury are quite different. This is the sort of acknowledgment that helps underwrite compatibilism, whether neutralist or affirming determinism.

[6] Bernard Williams, *Ethics and the Limits of Philosophy* (Cambridge: Harvard University Press), 1985, p. 38.

[7] See, for example, Bernard Williams, "Persons, Character, and Morality," "Moral Luck," "Internal and External Reasons," and "Practical Necessity," all reprinted in *Moral Luck* (Cambridge: Cambridge University Press, 1981).

[8] Richard Sorabji, *Necessity, Cause, and Blame,* (Ithaca: Cornell University Press, 1980), p. 267.

[9] Ibid., p. 267.

[10] Nancy Sherman, *The Fabric of Character* (Oxford: Clarendon Press, 1989), p. 172.

[11] Richard Sorabji, "Aristotle on the Role of Intellect in Virtue" in *Essays on Aristotle's Ethics,* ed. by Amélie Rorty (Berkeley: University of California Press, 1980), p. 216.

[12] Owen Flanagan, "Identity and Strong and Weak Evaluation," in *Identity, Character, and Morality,* p. 44.

[13] See Gary Watson, "Responsibility and the Limits of Evil," esp. pp. 274–75, in *Responsibility, Character, and the Emotions,* ed. Ferdinand Schoeman (New York: Cambridge University Press, 1987).

[14] Trianosky, "Natural Affection and Responsibility for Character," *Identity, Character, and Morality,* p. 104.

[15] Ibid., p. 104.
[16] Ibid., p. 105.
[17] Ibid., p. 99.
[18] Terence Irwin, *Aristotle's First Principles* (New York: Clarendon Press, 1992), pp. 373–74.
[19] Bernard Williams, "Practical Necessity," reprinted in *Moral Luck* (Cambridge: Cambridge University Press, 1981), p. 130.
[20] Bernard Williams, "Practical Necessity," p. 128.
[21] Ibid., p. 130.
[22] Ibid.
[23] Ibid.
[24] Williams's discussion in "Practical Necessity" does not directly concern ethics, and he is not there discussing incapacities of character mainly to make claims about responsibility for virtues and vices. Nevertheless, the basic elements of his analysis generally fit with the moral psychology presented here.
[25] Patricia Greenspan, "Unfreedom and Responsibility," reprinted in *Responsibility, Character, and the Emotions*, pp. 79–80.

Chapter 2. Ethical Disability and Responsibility

[1] Some of the main claims of this chapter are presented in less fully elaborated form in my "Taking Ethical Disability Seriously," in *Ratio* 11, no. 2 (1998): 141–58, and also in my "Luck and Retribution," in *Philosophy*, no. 74 (1999): 535–555.
[2] Immanuel Kant, *Foundations of the Metaphysics of Morals*, trans. by L. W. Beck (Indianapolis: Bobbs-Merrill, 1976), p. 20.
[3] Ibid., p. 21.
[4] Ibid., p. 4.
[5] J. S. Mill, *Utilitarianism*, ed. George Sher (Indianapolis: Hackett, 1979), p. 21.
[6] Kant also holds that: "Man (even the most wicked) does not, under any maxim whatsoever, repudiate the moral law in the manner of a rebel (renouncing obedience to it). The law, rather, forces itself upon him irresistibly by virtue of his moral predisposition; and were no other incentive working in opposition, he would adopt the law into his supreme maxim as the sufficient determining ground of his will; that is, he would be morally good. But by virtue of an equally innocent natural predisposition he depends upon the incentives of his sensuous nature and adopts them also (in accordance with the principle of self-love) into his maxim." *Religion Within the Limits of Reason Alone*, p. 31.
[7] John McDowell, "Are Moral Requirements Hypothetical Imperatives?" in *Proceedings of the Aristotelian Society*, supp. vol. 52 (Tisbury: Compton Press, 1978), p. 28.
[8] Ibid., p. 22.
[9] Ibid., p. 27.
[10] Ibid., p. 23.
[11] Kant, *Foundations of the Metaphysics of Morals*, p. 73.
[12] Ibid.
[13] Ibid.
[14] Ibid.
[15] Sarah Broadie, *Ethics With Aristotle* (New York: Oxford University Press, 1991), p. 161.
[16] Susan Wolf, *Freedom Within Reason* (New York: Oxford University Press, 1990), p. 75.
[17] Ibid., pp. 75–76.
[18] Ibid., p. 121–22.

[19] Michele Moody-Adams, "On the Old Saw That Character Is Destiny," in *Identity, Character, and Morality*, ed. Owen Flanagan and Amélie Oksenberg Rorty (Cambridge: MIT Press, 1990), p. 125.

[20] John McDowell, "Two Sorts of Naturalism," in *Virtues and Reasons*, ed. Rosalind Hursthouse, Gavin Lawrence, and Warren Quinn (Oxford: Clarendon Press, 1998), pp. 178–79.

[21] Thomas Reid, *Inquiry and Essays*, ed. Ronald E. Beanblossom and Keith Lehrer (Indianapolis: Hackett, 1983), p. 338.

[22] Ibid., p. 344.

[23] Ibid, pp. 343–44.

[24] Wolf, *Freedom Within Reason*, p. 81.

[25] Ibid.

[26] Susan Wolf, "Sanity and the Metaphysics of Responsibility," in *Responsibility, Character and the Emotions*, ed. Ferdinand Schoeman (New York: Cambridge University Press, 1987), p. 57.

[27] Ibid., p. 58.

[28] R. A. Duff argues that "blame is a kind of moral argument *with* another person. Blame is focused on and justified by the other's wrongdoing. It also aims, normally, to modify her attitudes and conduct:". R. A. Duff, *Trials and Punishments* (Cambridge: Cambridge University Press, 1986), p. 47. He also writes: "Moral blame should be understood as a response to another's wrong-doing which aims to persuade her to accept the moral judgment on that wrong-doing which it expresses, and thus to bring her to impose on herself the pain which belongs with guilt and remorse" (ibid., p. 60). His discussion has influenced my own, especially with respect to seeing blame as involving the wrongdoer in the process.

[29] Gilbert Harman, *The Nature of Morality* (New York: Oxford University Press, 1977), pp. 108–9.

[30] Ibid., p. 109.

[31] Duff also makes the comparison to admiration and gratitude, though the overall account of punishment that he gives puts more weight on its expressive and communicative dimension than does the sketch I give here. See his *Trials and Punishments*, esp. chap. 9.

[32] Both Thomas Aquinas and Thomas Reid argue that there are passions that follow judgment (rather than the other way round) and that there is a way, then, of seeing how even anger or resentment can be part of a correct response, and not just a feeling that is apt to disturb or impede sound judgment. See, for example, Aquinas, *De Malo*, Q. 12, art. 1, and Reid, *Essays on the Active Powers*, chap. 7, in *Inquiries and Essays*.

[33] Jean Hampton, "The Retributive Idea" in *Forgiveness and Mercy*, ed. Jeffrie G. Murphy and Jean Hampton (New York: Cambridge University Press, 1994), p. 133.

[34] Ibid., p. 132.

[35] Ibid.

[36] Joel Feinberg's "The Expressive Function of Punishment" has been an influential piece defending what I would regard as a quasi-retributivist justification of punitive sanction. I say "quasi-retributivist" because my own view is that retributivism should not be interpreted or explicated expressively or symbolically. Reprinted in *A Reader on Punishment*, ed. A. Duff and D. Garland (Oxford: Oxford University Press, 1994).

[37] Anthony Kenny discusses some of the most important and familiar metaphors used to make the case for retributivism (a case that he believes cannot be made successfully). See his *Free Will and Responsibility* (London: Routledge & Kegan Paul, 1988), chap. 4.

[38] Herbert Morris argues that retributivist justifications could be integrated into a paternalistic justification of punishment. I think that they could be but that they also have weight independent of any tie with paternalism. Morris does say that there are certain

(unmet) conditions for the applicability of his theory and any moral theory of punishment. "The first is that the norms addressed to persons are generally just and that the society is to some substantial extent one in which those who are liable to punishment have roughly equal opportunities to conform to those just norms. The second condition is equally important. The theory presupposes that there is a general commitment among persons to whom the norms apply to the values underlying them. If these two conditions are not met, we do not have what I understand as a practice of punishment for which any moral justification can be forthcoming." "A Paternalistic Theory of Punishment," reprinted in *Punishment and Rehabilitation*, ed. Jeffrie G. Murphy (Belmont: Wadsworth, 1995), p. 165. It would indeed be desirable to meet these conditions, but I think that a retributivist justification for punishment could be in place even if there were members of the society whose commitment to the values underlying its norms was only partial or the society's commitment to them was not as general or uniform as I suspect Morris intends. Some of my reasons for this are based upon my conception of ethical disability.

[39] Nigel Walker presents a number of arguments against retributivism, and in his culminating discussion writes: "This does not mean that retributivists are completely routed: only that they must retreat to ground where they are less open to attack—their right to have retributive feelings." Nigel Walker, *Why Punish?* (Oxford: Oxford University Press, 1991), p. 139. My point is that this is a mischaracterization of the relevant feelings, and that it misses the point of their aptness and significance.

[40] See Gary Watson, "Responsibility and the Limits of Evil: Variations on a Strawsonian Theme," in *Responsibility, Character, and the Emotions*, ed. Ferdinand Schoeman, 256–86 (New York: Cambridge University Press, 1987), esp. pp. 274–75, for discussion of this difficult issue.

Chapter 3. Ethical Accessibility and Plasticity of Character

[1] The comparison of Aristotle and Maimonides on character is one that I initially explored in "Plasticity and Perfection: Maimonides and Aristotle on Character," in *Religious Studies* 33 (1997): 443–54.

[2] We could say that for Maimonides the giving of the Law is grace, so there is supernatural agency in his ethics as well. However, once the Law is given, the extent to which human beings are virtuous is a matter of their own natural (if metaphysically dependent) causality. In that respect, he is closer to Aristotle than to Aquinas, and so the contrast between Maimonides and Aristotle can be particularly instructive. See Aquinas, *Summa Theologica*, especially Q. 109, articles 1–10. He argues that "man cannot fulfill all the divine commandments without healing grace" (art. 4), and "even a man who already possesses grace needs a further assistance of grace in order to live righteously" (art. 9).

[3] See Hume's *Enquiry*, part I, sec. 8. Hume writes: "A person of an obliging disposition gives a peevish answer: But he has not dined. A stupid fellow discovers an uncommon alacrity in his carriage: But he has met with a sudden piece of good fortune. Or even when an action, as sometimes happens, cannot be particularly accounted for, either by the person himself or by others; we know, in general, that the characters of men are to a certain degree inconstant and irregular." He makes this observation in the course of presenting an argument that people's characters tend to be stable and constant, though of course, people occasionally act out of character. *An Enquiry Concerning Human Understanding*, 3d ed., ed. L. A. Selby-Bigge (Oxford: Clarendon Press, 1975), p. 88.

[4] Immanuel Kant, *Religion Within the Limits of Reason Alone*, trans. Theodore M. Greene and Hoyt H. Hudson (New York: Harper & Row, 1960), p. 46.

[5] Ibid., p. 55.

[6] Maimonides, "Eight Chapters," in *Ethical Writings of Maimonides*, ed. and trans. by R. L. Weiss and C. Butterworth (New York: Dover, 1983), pp. 83–84. See also Maimonides, "Laws Relating to Moral Dispositions and to Ethical Conduct," in *Book of Knowledge*, trans. by Moses Hyamson (Jerusalem: Feldheim Publishers, 1981). Maimonides says therein, "Every human being is characterized by numerous moral dispositions which differ from each other and are exceedingly divergent." (chap. 1, 1) And, "Of all the various dispositions, some belong to one from the beginning of his existence and correspond to his physical constitution. Others are such that a particular individual's nature is favourably predisposed to them and prone to acquire them more rapidly than other traits. Others again are not innate but have been either learnt from others, or are self-originated, as the result of an idea that has entered the mind or, having heard that a certain disposition is good for him and should be cultivated by him, one trained himself in it till it became part of his nature" (chap. 1, 2).

[7] Maimonides, "Eight Chapters," p. 68.

[8] Ibid., p. 67. I should add that Maimonides distinguishes between wisdom and piety. The wise individual is the one with virtues, each of which lies in a mean. The pious person has characteristics that are extreme, in particular with regard to humility and anger. The pious person is not to feel anger but to always be tranquil. For the pious person, the extreme with respect to anger is not timidity or servility but tranquility. And the pious person is also to be very humble. The reason this is an issue for Maimonides (and in a way that it is not an issue for Aristotle) is that the religious tradition tells us to be holy; and so that we may be like God, we must strive to be free of passions. It is in Maimonides' "Laws Concerning Character Traits" that there is a clear statement of the standard of piety, in contrast with the standard of virtue. That work is part of *The Book of Knowledge*, which in turn is the first of the fourteen books of Maimonides' *Mishneh Torah.* See also Daniel Frank, "Anger as a Vice: A Maimonidean Critique of Aristotle's Ethics," *History of Philosophy Quarterly* 7:269–81, and his article "Humility as a Virtue: A Maimonidean Critique of Aristotle's Ethics," in *Moses Maimonides and His Time*, ed. Eric Ormsby (Washington, D.C.: Catholic University of America Press, 1989), pp. 89–99.

[9] See especially Maimonides, *The Guide for the Perplexed*, trans. M. Friedlander (New York: E. P. Dutton, 1910), bk. 3, chap. 54.

[10] Maimonides, "Eight Chapters," p. 84.

[11] Ibid.

[12] Ibid., p. 85.

[13] Ibid.

[14] Raymond L. Weiss, *Maimonides' Ethics* (Chicago: University of Chicago Press, 1991), p. 30.

[15] Maimonides, "Eight Chapters," p. 70.

[16] Maimonides, *Guide*, 3:36.

[17] See Maimonides' discussion of the issue of the rationality of commandments in *Guide*, 3:28. He says that even those "precepts concerning which people are in doubt, and of divided opinions, some believing that they are mere commands, and serve no purpose whatever" are such that they must have "some bearing upon one of the following three things, viz., the regulation of our opinions, or the improvement of our social relations, which implies two things, the removal of injustice, and the teaching of good morals."

[18] See, for example, Maimonides, *Guide*, 3:32, for Maimonides' account of how worship of God begins with a reliance upon rites and develops through stages of prayer and contemplation, as obedience and love of God become more theoretically perfected. This is suggested by Maimonides as an explanation for many of the laws. Of the many laws that

seem to have no contemporary relevance or whose rationales are obscure, he says that "God refrained from prescribing what the people by their natural disposition would be incapable of obeying, and gave the above-mentioned commandments as a means of securing His chief object, viz., to spread knowledge of Him [among the people], and to cause them to reject idolatry."

[19] R. A. Duff, *Trials and Punishments* (Cambridge: Cambridge University Press, 1986), p. 246.

[20] Michele Moody-Adams, "On the Old Saw That Character Is Destiny," p. 128.

[21] Herbert Morris, "A Paternalistic Theory of Punishment," reprinted in *Punishment and Rehabilitation*, 3d ed., ed. Jeffrie G. Murphy (Belmont: Wadsworth, 1995), p. 158.

[22] Ibid., p. 159.

[23] Maimonides, "Eight Chapters," p. 73.

[24] Immanuel Kant, *The Doctrine of Virtue*, trans. Mary J. Gregor (Philadelphia: University of Pennsylvania Press, 1964), p. 107.

[25] Maimonides, "Laws Relating to Moral Dispositions and to Ethical Conduct," chap. 6, 1, in *Book of Knowledge*.

[26] Ibid., chap. 6, 2.

[27] See Nancy Sherman, *The Fabric of Character* (Oxford: Clarendon Press, 1989), for an examination of the role of family, friends, and political life generally in the development of the virtues.

[28] See Jeffrie G. Murphy, "Hatred: A Qualified Defense." He writes: "Since I regard retributive hatred as in principle the natural, fitting, and proper response to certain instances of wrongdoing, I do not regard the passion itself as either immoral or irrational. (It is not the moral equivalent of a phobia.) I do, however, believe that it is generally both irrational and immoral to be led, to use Spinoza's phrase, by this dangerous and often blind passion." In *Forgiveness and Mercy*, ed. Jeffrie G. Murphy and Jean Hampton (Cambridge: Cambridge University Press, 1988), p. 108.

[29] In a passage bearing on whether there are ever moral grounds to regard an agent as incorrigible, R. A. Duff writes: "The point here is not that we can never have empirically adequate grounds for believing that punishment will not in fact bring a criminal to repentance: it is rather that we can never have *morally* adequate grounds—nothing could count as morally adequate grounds—for treating a person as being beyond redemption. We owe it to every moral agent to treat him as one who can be brought to reform and redeem himself—to keep trying, however vainly, to reach the good that is in him, and to appeal to his capacity for moral understanding and concern. To talk thus of "the good that is in him" is not to make some psychological claim to the effect that he "really" cares for the values which he flouts: it is rather to combine the conceptual claim that every moral agent has the capacity or potential for moral development and reform, with the moral claim that we should never give up hope of bringing him to actualise that potential" (*Trials and Punishments*, p. 266).

Chapter 4. Conscience and Its Work

[1] Sometimes, the deeply personal sense of conscience is expressed in a way that is not directly or primarily tied to morality. It may express the agent's sense of what he must do as a matter of pursuing the central project of his life. For example, before Gauguin left for the Pacific islands to pursue his art, his friends made him a banquet. Stéphane Mallarmé proposed the following toast: "Gentlemen, the most urgent matter before us is to drink to the return of Paul Gauguin, but not without admiring that superb conscience of his which,

in the brilliance of his talent, leads him to seek exile in faraway places and renewal within himself." Françoise Cachin, *Gauguin: The Quest for Paradise* (New York: Harry N. Abrams, 1992), p. 64.

[2] Joseph Butler, *Fifteen Sermons* (London: G. Bell & Sons, 1967), Sermon 2, sec. 8, p. 53.

[3] Ibid., Sermon 3, sec. 3, p. 63.

[4] Ibid.

[5] Immanuel Kant, *Religion Within the Limits of Reason Alone*, trans. Theodore M. Greene and Hoyt H. Hudson (New York: Harper & Row, 1960), p. 174.

[6] Ibid.

[7] Immanuel Kant, *Lectures on Ethics*, trans. L. Infield (Indianapolis: Hackett, 1963), p. 129.

[8] Immanuel Kant, *The Doctrine of Virtue*, trans. Mary J. Gregor (Philadelphia: University of Pennsylvania Press, 1964), p. 103.

[9] Ibid.

[10] Ibid., p. 60.

[11] Ibid., p. 61.

[12] J. S. Mill, *Utilitarianism* (Indianapolis: Hackett, 1979), p. 27.

[13] Ibid., p. 28.

[14] Ibid.

[15] Ibid., p. 27.

[16] Ibid., p. 30.

[17] Ibid.

[18] Adam Smith, *The Theory of Moral Sentiments*, ed. D. D. Raphael and A. L. Macfie (Indianapolis: Liberty Fund, 1984), p. 130.

[19] Thomas Reid, *Essays on the Active Powers of Man*, in *Inquiry and Essays*, ed. Ronald E. Beanblossom and Keith Lehrer (Indianapolis: Hackett, 1983), p. 355.

[20] Ibid., p. 322.

[21] Aquinas, *Summa Theologica*, Q. 94, art 1.

[22] Ibid., Q. 94, art. 2.

[23] Ibid., Q. 94, art. 6.

[24] Alan Donagan, *The Theory of Morality* (Chicago: University of Chicago Press, 1977), p. 134.

[25] Aquinas, *Summa Theologica*, Q. 94, art. 6.

[26] Mill, *Utilitarianism*, p. 30. Also, see G. A. Cohen's "Reason, Humanity, and the Moral Law" written in response to and printed along with Christine Korsgaard's 1992 Tanner Lectures in *The Sources of Normativity*. He constructs a case that illustrates this point and other points I have made. He writes:

> Consider an idealized Mafioso: I call him 'idealized' because an expert has told me that real Mafioso don't have the heroic attitude that my Mafioso displays. This Mafioso does not believe in doing unto others as you would have them do unto you: in relieving suffering just because it is suffering, in keeping promises because they are promises, in telling the truth because it is the truth, and so on. Instead, he lives by a code of strength and honour that matters as much to him as some of the principles I said he disbelieves in matter to most of us. And when he has to do some hideous thing that goes against his inclinations, and he is tempted to fly, he steels himself, and we can say of him, as much as of us, with the same exaggeration or lack of it, that he steels on pain of risking a loss of identity. *The Sources of Normativity* (Cambridge: Cambridge University Press, 1997), p. 183.

This may or may not be a bit of an idealization of a Mafioso, but it plausibly describes a certain type of ethical disability.

[27] Adam Smith, *The Theory of Moral Sentiments*, p. 176.

[28] Ibid., p. 134.

[29] Kant, *Lectures on Ethics*, p. 129.

[30] Ibid.

[31] Ibid., p. 130.

[32] Augustine, *Confessions*, trans., F. J. Sheed (New York: Sheed & Ward, 1942), bk. 10, 31, p. 195.

[33] Bernard Williams, "Practical Necessity," in *Moral Luck* (Cambridge: Cambridge University Press, 1981), p. 130.

[34] Michael S. Moore, "The Moral Worth of Retribution," reprinted in *Punishment and Rehabilitation*, 3d ed., ed. Jeffrie G. Murphy (Belmont: Wadsworth, 1995), p. 122.

[35] Adam Smith, *The Theory of Moral Sentiments*, p. 117.

[36] Thomas Reid, *Inquiry and Essays*, p. 355.

[37] David Hume, *A Treatise of Human Nature*, ed. L. A. Selby-Bigge (Oxford: Oxford University Press, 1978), 3.3.6, p. 619.

[38] Smith, *The Theory of Moral Sentiments*, p. 165.

[39] Reid, *Inquiry and Essays*, p. 358.

Chapter 5. Metaethics and Moral Psychology

[1] See Philippa Foot, *Virtues and Vices* (Berkeley: University of California Press, 1978). In her articles from the late 1950s, she develops the critique of noncognitivism and prescriptivism, on the way to beginning to reconstruct the virtues. See also R. M. Hare, *The Language of Morals* (Oxford: Oxford University Press, 1952). Also, *Freedom and Reason* (Oxford: Oxford University Press, 1963).

[2] G. E. M. Anscombe, "Modern Moral Philosophy," originally in *Philosophy* 33 (1958), and reprinted in volume 3 of *The Collected Papers of G. E. M. Anscombe* (Minneapolis: University of Minnesota Press, 1981), pp. 26–42. I shall add here, as an aside, that I suspect that part of what motivated the critiques developed by both Foot and Anscombe was the idea that the theories they were responding to implied that we do not *know* many moral matters that indeed we do know. If that is the case, then there must be something wrong with those theories.

[3] Iris Murdoch is also important in this regard. *The Sovereignty of Good* has been important to recent developments in moral realism because of the way in which she explored the texture of moral thought and sensibility in terms of the nature of attention to the world. Those essays explored some of the messy but familiar details of moral life instead of giving a theoretical account of morality in terms of something else (e.g., biological, psychological, or linguistic theory). *The Sovereignty of Good* (London: Ark Paperbacks, 1986).

[4] I do not mean that the views I describe are views that are to be attributed to Wittgenstein. They are views that it is appropriate to see as influenced by certain aspects of Wittgenstein's thought, even if they are the result of developing those influences in ways that are remote from Wittgenstein's own views. See his "A Lecture on Ethics," *Philosophical Review* 74 (1965): 3–11.

[5] J. L. Mackie's *Ethics: Inventing Right and Wrong* (Harmondsworth: Penguin Books, 1977), has been the most influential presentation of error theory. It is also important to recent versions of antirealism because of how seriously Mackie took the ways in which

"ordinary moral judgements include a claim to objectivity, an assumption that there are objective values" (p. 35). He, of course, sought to show that there are not objective values, but he argued that this could not be accomplished by linguistic or conceptual analysis. Thus, his error-theoretic skepticism has pushed antirealists to take specific moral concepts and the argumentative and reasoning practices in morality more seriously, in a way that is a counterpart to how Foot, Anscombe, and Murdoch influenced realists to do so.

[6] Simon Blackburn, "Errors and the Phenomenology of Value," in Blackburn, *Essays in Quasi-Realism* (New York: Oxford University Press, 1993), p. 156.

[7] Simon Blackburn, "How to Be an Ethical Antirealist," in *Essays in Quasi-Realism*, p. 172.

[8] Ibid.

[9] Ibid., p. 173.

[10] Blackburn, "Errors and the Phenomenology of Value," p. 160.

[11] Ibid., p. 155.

[12] Blackburn, "How to Be an Ethical Antirealist," p. 176.

[13] Ibid., p. 178.

[14] The argument, "If projectivism is true then it is possible that cruel actions are not wrong; but it is not possible that cruel actions are not wrong; so, projectivism is incorrect" was suggested as an illustration of my view by an anonymous reader. That reader is of course, not at fault if my argumentation is flawed. The overall argument of the chapter that projectivism cannot distinguish successfully between conative force (and thus leaves it open that cruelty might not be wrong) is a development of some of the claims in my "Metaethics and Teleology," which will appear in the *Review of Metaphysics* at the time this book goes to press.

[15] Blackburn, "Moral Realism," p. 122.

[16] Stephen Everson, "Aristotle and the explanation of evaluation: a reply to David Charles," in *Aristotle and Moral Realism*, ed. Robert Heinaman (Boulder: Westview Press), 1995, p. 198.

[17] T. H. Huxley, *Evolution and Ethics* (D. Appleton and Company, 1899), p. 30.

[18] Ibid., p. 79.

[19] Ibid., p. 80.

[20] Ibid., p. 82.

[21] John McDowell, "Values and Secondary Qualities," in *Essays on Moral Realism*, ed. Geoffrey Sayre-McCord (Ithaca: Cornell University Press, 1988), p. 167.

[22] Ibid., p. 168.

[23] Blackburn, "How to Be an Ethical Antirealist," p. 173.

[24] Blackburn, "Moral Realism," p. 129.

[25] In "Values and Secondary Qualities" John McDowell argues that a point against projectivism is that on projectivist bases, the superimposing of values onto a value neutral reality tends very strongly to become a search for a set of principles. This is the way in which we would need to understand the workings of the projective mechanism. In *Essays on Moral Realism*, see esp. pp. 179–80.

[26] Mark Platts, "Moral Reality," in *Essays on Moral Realism*, p. 299.

[27] My discussion here has been influenced by Stephen Everson's "Aristotle and the Explanation of Evaluation: A Reply to David Charles," in *Aristotle and Moral Realism*.

[28] Platts, "Moral Reality," pp. 292–293.

[29] Gary Watson, "On the Primacy of Character," chap. 19 in *Identity, Character, and Morality*, ed. Owen Flanagan and Amélie Oksenberg Rorty (Cambridge: MIT Press, 1990), p. 453.

[30] In discussion after presentation of a paper at the University of St. Andrews in which I defended some of these claims, John Broome pressed in particular on the matter of fair-

ness being specifiable in a general form and in a manner that can be determinative of judgment. The formulation I give here is close to the one he suggested. I am sure that I did not satisfy him in making a case for doubting that morality can be systematized. I do want to acknowledge his helpful insights and comments on this matter.

[31] Nancy Sherman, *Making a Necessity of Virtue* (New York: Cambridge University Press, 1997), p. 263.

Conclusion

[1] The point is made clearly in the following passage from Nagel's influential essay, "Moral Luck." "If one cannot be responsible for consequences of one's acts due to factors beyond one's control, or for antecedents of one's acts that are properties of temperament not subject to one's will, or for the circumstances that pose one's moral choices, then how can one be responsible even for the stripped-down acts of the will itself, if they are the product of antecedent circumstances outside of the will's control? The area of genuine agency, and therefore of legitimate moral judgment, seems to shrink under this scrutiny to an extensionless point." Thomas Nagel, "Moral Luck," in *Mortal Questions* (New York: Cambridge University Press, 1979), p. 35. See also Michele Moody-Adams's critique of Nagel's argument. "On the Old Saw That Character is Destiny," chapter 5 of *Identity, Character, and Morality*, ed. Flanagan and Rorty.

[2] Christine Korsgaard, *The Sources of Normativity* (Cambridge: Cambridge University Press, 1997), p. 129.

[3] Ibid., pp. 120–21.

[4] Aquinas, *Summa Theologica*, Q. 94, art. 2.

Bibliography

Anscombe, G. E. M. "Modern Moral Philosophy." In *The Collected Papers of G. E. M. Anscombe*, 3:26–42. Minneapolis: University of Minnesota Press, 1981.

Aquinas, Thomas. *Summa Theologica*. In *Introduction to St. Thomas Aquinas*, edited by Anton C. Pegis. New York: Random House, 1948.

——. *De Malo*. Translated by Jean Oesterle. Notre Dame: University of Notre Dame Press, 1995.

Aristotle. *Nicomachean Ethics*. Translated by Terence Irwin. Indianapolis: Hackett, 1985.

——. *Rhetoric*. In *The Basic Works of Aristotle*, edited by Richard McKeon. New York: Random House, 1941.

Augustine. *Confessions*. Translated by F. J. Sheed. New York: Sheed & Ward, 1942.

Blackburn, Simon. "Errors and the Phenomenology of Value." In *Essays in Quasi-Realism*. New York: Oxford University Press, 1993.

——. "How to Be an Ethical Antirealist." In *Essays in Quasi-Realism*. New York: Oxford University Press, 1993.

——. "Moral Realism." In *Essays in Quasi-Realism*. New York: Oxford University Press, 1993.

Broadie, Sarah. *Ethics with Aristotle*. New York: Oxford University Press, 1991.

Butler, Joseph. *Fifteen Sermons*. London: G. Bell & Sons, 1967.

Cachin, Francoise. *Gauguin: The Quest for Paradise*. New York: Harry N. Abrams, 1992.

Cohen, G. A. "Reason, Humanity, and the Moral Law." In *The Sources of Normativity*. Cambridge: Cambridge University Press, 1997.

Donagan, Alan. *The Theory of Morality*. Chicago: University of Chicago Press, 1977.

Duff, R. A. *Trials and Punishments*. Cambridge: Cambridge University Press, 1986.

Everson, Stephen. "Aristotle and the Explanation of Evaluation: A Reply to David Charles." In *Aristotle and Moral Realism*, edited by Robert Heinaman, 173–99. Boulder: Westview Press, 1995.

141

Feinberg, Joel."The Expressivist Function of Punishment." In *A Reader on Punishment*, edited by A. Duff and D. Garland. Oxford: Oxford University Press, 1994.

Flanagan, Owen. "Identity and Strong and Weak Evaluation." In *Identity, Character, and Morality*, edited by Owen Flanagan and Amélie Oksenberg Rorty, 37–65. Cambridge: MIT Press, 1990.

Foot, Philippa. *Virtues and Vices*. Berkeley: University of California Press, 1978.

Frank, Daniel. "Anger as a Vice: A Maimonidean Critique of Aristotle's Ethics." *History of Philosophy Quarterly* 7 (1990): 269–81.

———. "Humility as a Virtue: A Maimonidean Critique of Aristotle's Ethics." In *Moses Maimonides and His Time*, edited by Eric Ormsby. Washington, D.C.: Catholic University of America Press, 1989.

Greenspan, Patricia. "Unfreedom and Responsibility." In *Responsibility, Character, and the Emotions*, edited by Ferdinand Schoeman, 63–80. New York: Cambridge University Press, 1987.

Hampton, Jean. "The Retributive Idea." In *Forgiveness and Mercy*, edited by Jeffrie G. Murphy and Jean Hampton, 111–61. New York: Cambridge University Press, 1994.

Hare, R. M. *Freedom and Reason*. Oxford: Oxford University Press, 1963.

———. *The Language of Morals*. Oxford: Oxford University Press, 1952.

Harman, Gilbert. *The Nature of Morality*. New York: Oxford University Press, 1977.

Hume, David. *An Enquiry concerning Human Understanding*. 3d ed. Edited by L. A. Selby-Bigge. Oxford: Clarendon Press, 1975.

———. *A Treatise of Human Nature*. Edited by L. A. Selby-Bigge. Oxford: Oxford University Press, 1978.

Huxley, T. H. *Evolution and Ethics*. New York: D. Appleton, 1899.

Irwin, Terence. *Aristotle's First Principles*. New York: Clarendon Press, 1992.

Jacobs, Jonathan. "Luck and Retribution." *Philosophy* 74 (1999): 335–55.

———. "Metaethics and Teleology." *Review of Metaphysics*, forthcoming.

———. "Plasticity and Perfection: Maimonides and Aristotle on Character." *Religious Studies* 33 (1997): 443–54.

———. "Taking Ethical Disability Seriously." *Ratio* 11 (1998): 141–58.

———. "The Virtues of Externalism." *Southern Journal of Philosophy* 34 (1996): 285–99.

Kant, Immanuel. *The Doctrine of Virtue*. Translated by Mary J. Gregor. Philadelphia: The University of Pennsylvania Press, 1964.

———. *Foundations of the Metaphysics of Morals*. Translated by L. W. Beck. Indianapolis: Bobbs-Merrill, 1976.

———. *Lectures on Ethics*. Translated by Louis Enfield. Indianapolis: Hackett, 1963.

———. *Religion Within the Limits of Reason Alone*, New York: Harper & Row, 1960.

Kenny, Anthony. *Freewill and Responsibility*. London: Routledge & Kegan Paul, 1988.

Korsgaard, Christine. *The Sources of Normativity*. Cambridge: Cambridge University Press, 1997.

Mackie, J. L. *Ethics: Inventing Right and Wrong*. Harmondsworth: Penguin Books, 1977.

Maimonides, Moses. "Eight Chapters." In *Ethical Writings of Maimonides*, edited and translated by R. L. Weiss and C. Butterworth, 59–104. New York: Dover, 1983.
——. *The Guide for the Perplexed*. Translated by M. Friedlander. New York: E. P. Dutton, 1910.
——. "Laws of Repentance." In *The Book of Knowledge*, translated by Moses Hyamson. Jerusalem: Feldheim, 1981.
——. "Laws Relating to Moral Dispositions and to Ethical Conduct." In *The Book of Knowledge*, translated by Moses Hyamson. Jerusalem: Feldheim, 1981.
McDowell, John. "Are Moral Requirements Hypothetical Imperatives?" In *Proceedings of the Aristotelian Society* (1978): 13–29. Supplementary Volume 52.
——. "Projection and Truth in Ethics." In *Moral Discourse and Practice*, edited by Stephen Darwall, Allan Gibbard, and Peter Railton, 215–25. New York: Oxford University Press, 1997.
——. "Two Sorts of Naturalism." In *Virtues and Reasons*, edited by Rosalind Hursthouse, Gavin Lawrence, and Warren Quinn, 149–79. Oxford: Clarendon Press, 1998.
——. "Values and Secondary Qualities." In *Essays on Moral Realism*, edited by Geoffrey Sayre-McCord. Ithaca: Cornell University Press, 1988.
Mill, John Stuart. *Utilitarianism*. Edited by George Sher. Indianapolis: Hackett, 1979.
Moody-Adams, Michele. 1990. "On the Old Saw That Character Is Destiny." In *Identity, Character, and Morality*, edited by Owen Flanagan and Amélie Oksenberg Rorty, 111–31. Cambridge: MIT Press, 1990.
Moore, Michael. "The Moral Worth of Retribution." In *Punishment and Rehabilitation*, 3d ed., edited by Jeffrie G. Murphy. Belmont: Wadsworth, 1995.
Morris, Herbert. "A Paternalistic Theory of Punishment." In *Punishment and Rehabilitation*, 3d ed., edited by Jeffrie G. Murphy, 154–68. Belmont: Wadsworth, 1995.
Murdoch, Iris. *The Sovereignty of Good*. London: Ark Paperbacks, 1986.
Murphy, Jeffrie G. "Hatred: A Qualified Defense." In *Forgiveness and Mercy*, edited by Jeffrie G. Murphy and Jean Hampton, 88–110. Cambridge: Cambridge University Press, 1988.
Nagel, Thomas. "Moral Luck." In *Mortal Questions*. New York: Cambridge University Press, 1979.
Platts, Mark. "Moral Reality." In *Essays on Moral Realism*, edited by Geoffrey Sayre-McCord. Ithaca: Cornell University Press, 1988.
Reid, Thomas. *Inquiry and Essays*. Edited by Ronald E. Beanblossom and Keith Lehrer. Indianapolis: Hackett, 1983.
Sherman, Nancy. *The Fabric of Character*. Oxford: Clarendon Press, 1989.
——. *Making a Necessity of Virtue*. New York: Cambridge University Press, 1997.
Smith, Adam. *The Theory of Moral Sentiments*. Edited by D. D. Raphael and A. L. MacFie. Indianapolis: Liberty Fund, 1984.
Sorabji, Richard. "Aristotle on the Role of the Intellect in Virtue." In *Essays on Aristotle's Ethics*, edited by Amélie Rorty. Berkeley: University of California Press, 1980.
——. *Necessity, Cause, and Blame*. Ithaca: Cornell University Press, 1980.

Trianosky, Gregory. "Natural Affection and Responsibility for Character." In *Identity, Character, and Morality,* edited by Owen Flanagan and Amélie Oksenberg Rorty, 93–109. Cambridge: MIT Press, 1990.

Walker, Nigel. *Why Punish?* Oxford: Oxford University Press, 1991.

Watson, Gary. "On the Primacy of Character." In *Identity, Character, and Morality,* edited by Owen Flanagan and Amélie Oksenberg Rorty, 449–69. Cambridge: MIT Press, 1990.

——. "Responsibility and the Limits of Evil: Variations on a Strawsonian Theme." In *Responsibility, Character, and the Emotions,* edited by Ferdinand Schoeman, 256–86. New York: Cambridge University Press, 1987.

Weiss, Raymond. *Maimonides' Ethics.* Chicago: University of Chicago Press, 1991.

Wiggins, David. "Truth, Invention and the Meaning of Life." In *Needs, Values, Truth,* 87–138. Oxford: Blackwell, 1987.

Williams, Bernard. *Ethics and the Limits of Philosophy.* Cambridge: Harvard University Press, 1985.

——. "Practical Necessity." In *Moral Luck,* 124–31. Cambridge: Cambridge University Press, 1981.

Wittgenstein, Ludwig. "A Lecture on Ethics." *Philosophical Review* 74 (1965): 3–11.

Wolf, Susan. *Freedom within Reason.* New York: Oxford University Press, 1990.

——. "Sanity and the Metaphysics of Responsibility." In *Responsibility, Character, and the Emotions,* edited by Ferdinand Schoeman, 46–62. New York: Cambridge University Press, 1987.

Wood, Ledger. "The Free-will Controversy." *Philosophy* 16 (1941): 386–99.

Index